Diving & Snorkeling
Guam & Yap

Tim Rock

LONELY PLANET PUBLICATIONS
Melbourne • Oakland • London • Paris

Diving & Snorkeling Guam & Yap
- A Lonely Planet Pisces Book

2nd Edition – January, 1999
1st Edition – 1994, Gulf Publishing Company

Published by
Lonely Planet Publications
192 Burwood Road, Hawthorn, Victoria 3122, Australia

Other offices
150 Linden Street, Oakland, California 94607, USA
10A Spring Place, London NW5 3BH, UK
1 rue du Dahomey, 75011 Paris, France

Photographs
by Tim Rock & Stephanie Brendl

Front cover photograph
Truck in cargo of the *Shoun Maru,* Rota, by Tim Rock

Back cover photographs
by Tim Rock

ISBN 0 86442 744 1

text and maps © Lonely Planet 1999
photographs © photographers as indicated 1999
shipwreck illustrations courtesy of U.S. National Park
Service, Submerged Cultural Resources Unit

Printed by H&Y Printing Ltd., Hong Kong

Contents

Diving in Rota   81

Overview of Yap   89

Yap Practicalities   92

Activities & Attractions   97

Author

Tim Rock

Tim Rock is an internationally published photojournalist who specializes in underwater exploration. Based on Guam, Rock has traveled Micronesia and the Indo-Pacific for nearly two decades. He is the author of numerous dive guides on the region, including Pisces' *Diving & Snorkeling Guide to Palau*, *Truk Lagoon* and *Bali and the Komodo Region*. He produced the ACE award finalist Aquaquest Micronesia Television series and has won awards from the AP, UPI and NPPA for writing and photography.

From the Author

A special thanks to Pete and Linda Peterson on Guam who have been strong supporters of many of my personal projects. Pete is without a doubt Guam's pioneer underwater explorer. The same to Mark and Lynn Michael of Rota who have been good for diving and good for Rota. Many thanks also to Bill Acker, his family and his staff at Yap Divers. Bill has been tireless in bringing the word of Yap's undersea beauty to the world.

Photography notes

Tim Rock uses Nikonos RSAF Cameras and Nikon SB 104 & 105 strobes as his main photographic equipment. He also houses Nikon cameras in Aquatica housings used primarily for close-up and extreme wide angle work. In addition, the trusty Nikonos II, II and V cameras are part of his work force. On land, he uses Nikon F5 cameras with a variety of Nikon lenses. Film used is primarily Fujichrome Velvia, Provia and for special applications Ektachrome 200SW.

From the Publisher

The first edition of this book was published by Gulf Publishing Company. This second edition was produced in Lonely Planet's U.S. office. Roslyn Bullas is the Pisces Books publishing manager. Debra Miller edited this book. Henia Miedzinski handled the layout, with help from Hugh D'Andrade, who created the series design. Senior cartographer Alex Guilbert and Bart Wright —our fish cartos—drew the maps. Thanks to Scott Summers for his patience and production wisdom. Portions of the text were adapted from Lonely Planet's *Micronesia*. William Alevizon reviewed the manuscript for scientific accuracy. Special thanks to Tim Rock for answering queries in the middle of a tidal wave.

Lonely Planet Pisces Books

Lonely Planet acquired the Pisces line of diving and snorkeling books in 1997. The series will be developed and substantially revamped over the next few years and new titles will be added. We invite your comments and suggestions.

Pisces Pre-Dive Safety Guidelines

Before embarking on a scuba diving, skin diving or snorkeling trip, careful consideration should be given to a safe as well as enjoyable experience. You should:

- Possess a current diving certification card from a recognized scuba diving instructional agency (if scuba diving)
- Be sure you are healthy and feel comfortable diving
- Obtain reliable information about physical and environmental conditions at the dive site (e.g. from a reputable local dive operation)
- Be aware of local laws, regulations, and etiquette about marine life and environment
- Dive at sites within your experience level; if available, engage the services of a competent, professionally trained dive instructor or dive master

Underwater conditions vary significantly from one region, or even site, to another. Seasonal changes can significantly alter any site and dive conditions. These differences influence the way divers dress for a dive and what diving techniques they use.

Regardless of location, there are special requirements for diving in that area. Before your dive, ask about the environmental characteristics that can affect your diving and how local, trained divers deal with these considerations.

Warning & Request

Even with dive guides, things change – dive site conditions, regulations, topside information. Nothing stays the same for long. Your feedback on this book will be used to help update future editions and help make the next edition more useful. Excerpts from your correspondence may appear in our newsletter, Planet Talk, or in the Postcards section of our website, so please let us know if you don't want your letter published or your name acknowledged.

Correspondence can be addressed to:
Lonely Planet Publications
Pisces Books
150 Linden Street
Oakland, CA 94607

e-mail: pisces@lonelyplanet.com

Introduction

TIM ROCK

The intent of this guidebook is to introduce divers to the most popular and unique dive sites of Guam, Rota and Yap. Each site is described in terms of logistical requirements, typical depth, site features, common marine life and suggested diving experience, so you can find dive sites that complement your interests and abilities. Approximate dive positions are shown on maps in each section.

The undersea terrain of Guam, Rota and Yap is not known for its sea fans and soft corals as are the reefs and shipwrecks of nearby Truk (Chuuk) and Palau. But these islands can aptly be described as Micronesia's hard coral kingdoms. Some 400 species of coral inhabit these incredible and often overlooked reefs that are packed with over 900 species of fish and a plethora of invertebrates.

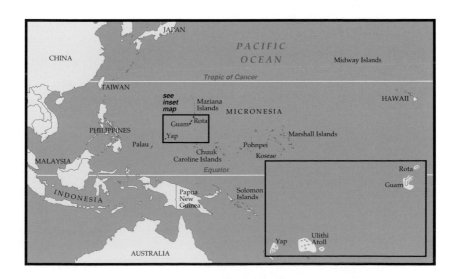

Diving hard corals requires a keen eye as fish and invertebrates take refuge or make homes in the nooks and crannies. Observant divers will find a great variety of fish—many in colorful juvenile stages—along with a broad range of anemones.

This is not to say these islands don't have drop-offs, fans and soft corals. The diving along Yap's Gilman Tip, Lionfish Wall and Yap Caverns ranks among the top attractions in Micronesia. Guam's Hospital Point and Orote Peninsula, sheer, blue and deep, are virtually unrivalled for water clarity. Rota's caves and points are breathtaking and Rota is said to have the clearest waters in the Pacific.

This region is blessed with a great variety of fish life. It is not unusual to see dolphins, large sharks, barracuda schools, manta rays, bumphead parrotfish, Napoleon wrasse, crevalle jacks, eagle rays, grunts, groupers and scores of reef tropicals during the course of a week's diving. In fact, Yap's Miil Channel is so rich in sea life you can see all of the above on one dive, with the exception of the dolphins, but they may join the boat on the way back.

There are, of course, numerous dive sites at each island. This is not intended to be a complete travel guide, but a clear overview of the dive potential at each locale and a listing of the better sites for the general diving public.

Sunset over Guam's Piti Bay and the Fish Eye Undersea Observatory.

Overview of Guam

TIM ROCK

Guam is a diverse and eclectic place. It is a veritable melting pot of Micronesian, Carolinian and Asian cultures, mixed with all the trappings of American life. Fast food restaurants, 1-hour photo shops and movie theaters line the roads.

On a drive around the island you could find yourself in a traffic jam on a six-lane highway at rush hour. But, half an hour later, you could be rolling down a traffic-free road enjoying scenic hills and valleys, populated only with coconut palms and flowing swordgrasses. On half the island, the only traffic to watch out for is the occassional local riding a carabao down a quiet village street.

Many people in the U.S. military consider Guam to be one of the best duty stations available, but Guam also has a large civilian population of around 120,000. A major player in the Asian tourist market, Guam is the "Caribbean of Japan," attracting over a million Japanese visitors annually. For those who love the sea and the outdoors, Guam is the place. Not only does Guam have a luxurious tropical atmosphere, but its central business district bustles with all the amenities found stateside. Its agricultural areas in the north and south feature historic villages nestled in the quiet hills and valleys.

TIM ROCK

Carabao were traditionally used for farming but at the on-set of WWII, many were set free and still roam in the wild today. Some ranchers keep them as pets.

History

Guam's first inhabitants, the Chamorros, lived on the Mariana Islands as early as 1500 BC. Believed to have migrated from Indonesia, they shared a language and cultural similarities with South-East Asians.

The first Western contact in the Pacific islands was on March 6, 1521 when the *Trinidad*, captained by Ferdinand Magellan, sailed into Guam's Umatac Bay. When the Spaniards left a few days later, they had killed seven Chamorros and burned 40 houses while retrieving a stolen rowboat. Forty years later, Miguel Lopez de Legazpi arrived and officially claimed the Marianas as a Spanish colony. For the next 250 years Spanish galleons stopped at Guam to take on provisions during annual runs between Manila and Acapulco. Jesuit missionaries attempted to convert the Chamorros to Catholicism. Resistance was met with armed force, and by the early 18th century, the Chamorro population had dropped to around 5000.

Spanish soldiers and Filipino men, brought in to help repopulate the islands, intermarried with Chamorro women, marking the end of the pure Chamorro bloodline.

WWII guns at Gaan Point's War in the Pacific National Memorial Park.

Following Spain's defeat in the Spanish-American War of 1898, Guam was ceded to the U.S. with the signing of the Treaty of Paris. For the next 40 years the U.S. maintained a largely unfortified naval control over the island.

On December 10, 1941, two days after the attack on Pearl Harbor, Japanese forces successfully invaded Guam. Toward the end of Japanese control the military rule became quite harsh. Guamanians were placed in work camps and subjected to forced labor.

The U.S. invasion began on July 17, 1944. A few days later some 55,000 U.S. troops hit Guam's beaches. Three weeks later the U.S. secured Guam after fierce fighting, which resulted in 17,500 Japanese and 7000 U.S. casualties. The capital city of Agana was in ruins and many smaller villages were also destroyed.

After WWII ended, the U.S. turned the military bases into permanent facilities. Today the U.S. presence in Guam is strong, with military facilities dominating the landscape and more than 23,000 military personnel and dependents on the island. Guam is an Unincorporated Territory of the U.S. Guamanians are U.S. citizens and have a civilian government.

Geography

Guam is the southernmost island in the Marianas chain, 30 miles long and only nine miles at its widest. Still, it is the largest island in Micronesia. The northern part of Guam is largely a raised limestone plateau, while the south is a mix of high volcanic hills and valleys with rivers and falls spilling into the sea. In the south is a barrier reef.

Reef formations surround much of the island. The beaches on the west side tend to be calmer, while those on the east coast have heavier seas. The southern tip of the island has a number of protected bays.

Mariana Trench

The Mariana Trench is an underwater canyon that extends 1,835 miles along the floor of the Pacific to the east of the Mariana Islands. At 38,635 ft, the trench contains the world's greatest known ocean depth.

The Mariana Islands, which are but the emerged tips of massive underwater mountains, can also make claim to another record. If measured from their bases deep in the Mariana Trench, the islands, which rise from the ocean floor more than 10,000 ft higher than Mt. Everest, would constitute the highest mountains in the world.

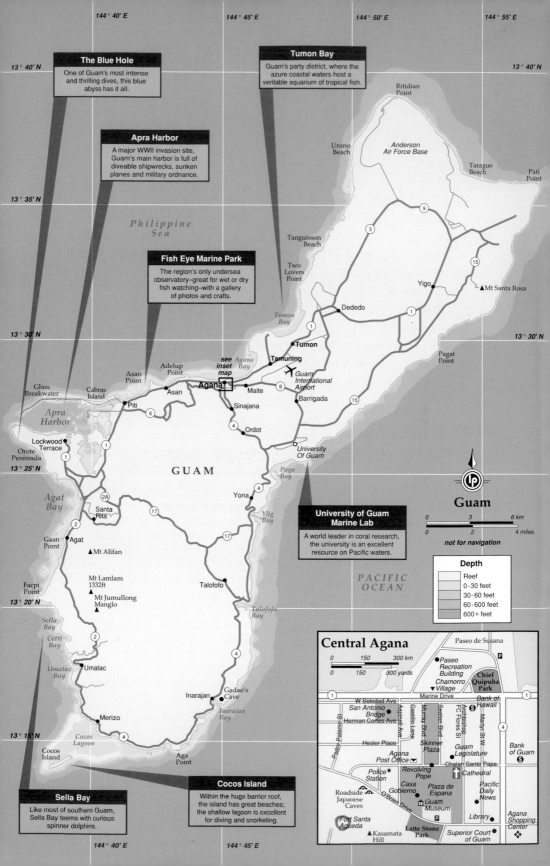

The Blue Hole
One of Guam's most intense and thrilling dives, this blue abyss has it all.

Tumon Bay
Guam's party district, where the azure coastal waters host a veritable aquarium of tropical fish.

Apra Harbor
A major WWII invasion site, Guam's main harbor is full of diveable shipwrecks, sunken planes and military ordnance.

Fish Eye Marine Park
The region's only undersea observatory–great for wet or dry fish watching–with a gallery of photos and crafts.

University of Guam Marine Lab
A world leader in coral research, the university is an excellent resource on Pacific waters.

Sella Bay
Like most of southern Guam, Sella Bay teems with curious spinner dolphins.

Cocos Island
Within the huge barrier roof, the island has great beaches; the shallow lagoon is excellent for diving and snorkeling.

Guam

not for navigation

Depth
- Reef
- 0 - 30 feet
- 30 - 60 feet
- 60 - 600 feet
- 600+ feet

Central Agana

Map labels:

144° 40' E, 144° 45' E, 144° 50' E, 144° 55' E
13° 40' N, 13° 35' N, 13° 30' N, 13° 25' N, 13° 20' N, 13° 15' N

Ritidian Point, Urono Beach, Anderson Air Force Base, Tarague Beach, Pati Point, Tanguisson Beach, Two Lovers Point, Yigo, Mt Santa Rosa, Dededo, Pagat Point, Tumon, Tamuning, Guam International Airport, Barrigada, Agana Bay, Adelup Point, Asan Point, Agana, Maite, Sinajana, Ordot, University Of Guam, Pago Bay, Yona, Ylig Bay, Asan, Piti, Cabras Island, Glass Breakwater, Apra Harbor, Lockwood Terrace, Orote Peninsula, Santa Rita, GUAM, Mt Alifan, Mt Lamlam 1332ft, Mt Jumullong Manglo, Talofofo, Talofofo Bay, Agat, Gaan Point, Agat Bay, Facpi Point, Sella Bay, Cetti Bay, Umatac Bay, Umatac, Inarajan, Gadao's Cave, Inarajan Bay, Merizo, Cocos Lagoon, Cocos Island, Aga Point

Philippine Sea, PACIFIC OCEAN, Tumon Bay, Pago Bay

Central Agana inset:
Paseo de Susana, Paseo Recreation Building, Chamorro Village, Chief Quipuha Park, Marine Drive, Bank of Hawaii, W Soledad Ave, San Antonio Bridge, Herman Cortes Ave, Aspinall Ave, Castille Lane, Murray Blvd, Seaton Blvd, FC Flores St, Archbishop Flores St, Martyr St, Hesler Place, Skinner Plaza, Guam Legislature, Chalan Santo Papa, Agana Post Office, Revolving Pope, Cathedral, Casa Gobierno, Plaza de Espana, Pacific Daily News, Police Station, Roadside Japanese Caves, Guam Museum, Library, Bank of Guam, Agana Shopping Center, Fort Santa Agueda, Kasamata Hill, Latte Stone Park, Superior Court of Guam, Pacific/Palomo St, O'Brien Drive

Guam
Practicalities

TIM ROCK

Climate

Guam's climate holds little in the way of surprises. Uniformly warm and humid, the evening
temperatures average 74°F (23°C) in the
evenings and 88°F (32°C) during the day. Dry season and trade wind season runs from late December to May. June through September features
calm seas, a slight breeze and scattered daily showers. Guam lies in the
typhoon belt and big storms come most frequently in the last half of the year.
Expect strong rains in October and November

The windward (eastern) side of Guam and the offshore reefs is most accessible during the summer months when the seas are glassy calm and flat. The
western side of the island, especially the Agat Bay and points south, is protected most of the year and good for diving. Visibility is affected by runoff,
so rainy season months mean lower visibility. Tides do not vary greatly on
Guam but visibility is best at high morning incoming tide. Currents can be
strong along the deep outer reef sites.

Water here is tropical, averaging about 80°F (27°C) and a dive skin is suit-
able for warmth and protection from abrasions or stings.

Language

English and Chamorro are the official languages, although English is spoken
by all. The Filipino, Japanese, Chinese, Korean and Micronesian communities are also strongly represented on Guam.

Getting There

Getting to Guam is not a problem. Guam is served daily by major carriers from
all over the Asian region and from the U.S. through Honolulu and Guam's $50
million A.B. Won Pat Guam International Air Terminal with connections to
most major cities. Guam's main carrier is Continental Micronesia.

Getting Around

Taxis can be quite pricey on Guam. It is best to rent a car while visiting, which is easy as all of the major rental agencies are here. **Professional Sports Divers** has a hotel/dive package, and will pick up at the airport and provide transport to the dive shop and marina. Do not depend on the bus system.

Entry

A valid U.S. passport is required to enter Guam, even for U.S. citizens. U.S. citizens can stay as long as they want. All non-U.S. citizens require a U.S. visa to visit Guam. There is a liberal visa waiver program that allows up to 15-day (only) stays. Check with the **Guam Visitor's Bureau**'s website at www.visitguam.org to see if your country participates.

Money

The U.S. dollar is the standard rate of currency. All major credit cards are widely accepted on Guam.

TIM ROCK

Para-sailing above Cocos Island Lagoon.

Time

Guam, Rota and Yap are located on the western side of the international dateline. Coming from Hawaii or points east you lose a day when crossing the international dateline. Guam, Rota and Yap are 10 hours ahead of GMT/UTC. When it's noon on Guam, it is the same time in Sydney, 6 pm the day before in San Francisco, and 1 pm the day before in London.

Electricity

Electricity is 110/120 volts, 60 cycles and the flat, two-pronged plug is used, the same as in the U.S. Some major hardware stores sell adapters for 220V but it is best to bring one with you if you need it, as stocks of such items are not always reliable.

Weights & Measures

The imperial system of measurement is used. Distances are in inches, feet, yards, miles. Weights are in ounces, pounds, tons. Air on scuba gauges is read in pounds and underwater depth is read in feet. See the conversion chart in the back of the book for metric equivalents.

What to Bring

General Supplies You can get anything on Guam as far as basic living goes. Prices are similar to those in Hawaii. There are some discount stores like **Cost-U-Less** and **K-Mart** that have batteries, some films, etc. Lightweight clothing is available at all clothing stores. Bring necessities like prescription medicines and items specific to your lifestyle.

Dive Related Equipment Guam is well-stocked for equipment and offers fine repair facilities. **Micronesia Divers Association** is a major regional wholesaler and you'll find a wide range of equipment for sale on the island. Rota and Yap also keep a good rental supply on hand. Technical diving equipment is also becoming more common and a couple of shops on Guam specialize in training and air fills. Water here is warm and dive skins and thin wetsuits are used mostly for protection from sunburn, coral cuts, stings and other minor marine hazards.

What to Wear

Dress is casual and island wear is always acceptable, whatever the occasion. Light summer clothing is appropriate, but keep in mind that the chill of an air-conditioned interior may require a light sweater. On the boat, the sun is hot and water reflective. Bring high-factor suntan lotion, a hat and perhaps a long-sleeved T-shirt. A light rain poncho is handy to protect against the chill of showers and fits handily into a dive bag.

Underwater Photography

TIM ROCK

Guam has one major professionally stocked camera store, **Kimura Camera** located in the ITC building. **Tropical Color**, just across the street, has dependable E-6 processing at reasonable prices. Film can be mounted or unmounted.

Some Nikonos equipment is available on Guam but underwater photographers should bring back-ups if possible. Housing sales and stock are limited to a couple of stores. Film is available but bring your own to ensure the kind of results you seek.

Digital videotape, Hi8 tape and video camera batteries are available at some photo stores and at **GAVIC**, the major Sony dealer. Prices are high. Some styles of video cameras, especially Sony and Canon, are available.

Business Hours

Most businesses are generally open 10 am to 7 pm and many are open until 10 pm. Bars are open until 1 or 2 am on weekdays and 4 am on weekends.

Accommodations

Luxurious international-standard hotels are set in landscaped gardens on the beaches of Tumon Bay, the island's premier resort destination. A few hotels are also located in the southern and central parts of the island. A number of fine business hotels and family-style accommodations are located in Agana, Maite, Tamuning and just minutes away from the air terminal.

Although scuba diving—especially introductory dives for Japanese tourists—is popular, there is only one hotel that offers dive/hotel packages for the experienced, traveling diver. **Inn on the Bay** operates in conjunction with Professional Sports Divers (in Agat Village) to provide boat dives leaving from Agat Marina.

Tipping is the same as in the rest of the U.S. Some hotels add a 10% service charge to the restaurant bill, so additional tipping is optional. The standard rate for restaurant service, taxi drivers, and hotel service personnel is 10 to 15%.

Dining & Food

Guam is a haven of the culinary arts. Despite the island's relatively small population, a wide array of restaurants offer scrumptious delicacies to warm any palate. Major hotels and restaurants serve high-quality, continental meals; many offer exotic ethnic dishes, as well.

A variety of fresh seafood is available, although little of it is caught here. Fresh fish, octopus and lobster are served either grilled or baked with vegetables, fruit or sashimi (raw tuna fish).

Travelers who venture farther into Guam will find innumerable Chamorro, Japanese, Korean, Thai, Vietnamese, Filipino, Chinese, Mexican and European restaurants, each with its own distinct ambiance. Of course, American fast food chains have become standard fare for those on the go.

Shopping

Shopping on Guam can help you decorate your home or enlarge your wardrobe with some of the finest purchases found in this part of the Pacific Rim. Try Guam's **Chamorro Village** shopping center for an array of ethnic arts. The Micronesia Mall brings more trendy fare and Guam's Tumon Bay is loaded with duty free and designer labels.

Illegal Items Guam laws basically mirror California state laws and U.S. federal laws. Tobacco and alcohol are the only legal drugs. Importation and possession of turtle shell and other endangered species items is also illegal.

Customs checks are performed upon entry to Guam. Visitors are allowed to bring three cartons of cigarettes, three bottles of spirits and reasonable amounts of perfume for personal use into duty-free Guam.

Guam Activities & Attractions

TIM ROCK

The capital city of Agana (pronounced a-GHAN-nya) has been the center of Guam since the Spanish period. With its parks and historic sites it's a pleasant place to spend a few hours sightseeing. If you have a car, it's easiest to park in the public lot south of the Cathedral; from there you can visit most of the sights on foot.

Tumon Bay, the tourist center of Guam, has all the usual attributes of resort life. The fringing white sand beach is lined with hotels, clubs and restaurants. Duty-free shops, shooting galleries and other tourist-targeted businesses prevail along the inland side of the road.

Guam attracts over a million tourists annually. As it is said to be summer all year round, you'll find all types of watersports, tours and night

The Sounds of Silence

A hike through Guam's rainforest is a safe but unusual experience. The jungles here are relatively quiet; plant life is abundant but animal and bird life is minimal. The fauna has been greatly reduced due to super-typhoons, human development and introduced species over the past 30 years. Poaching and wildfires have also contributed, reducing the numbers of native birds, deer and fruit bats on the island.

The biggest headline maker is the brown tree snake, which is native to the Solomon Islands and was accidentally introduced to Guam with military cargo in the 1940s. The snake has no natural enemies on Guam, a similar situation to that of Hawaii, with its introduced mongoose. The snake's initial food supply—mainly snails—was eventually depleted and so it began preying on birds. Land-based birds were most severely affected. The tree snake poses little danger to humans. Its toxin is mild and its nocturnal habits make sightings rare.

The brown tree snake's impact on the native ecology has left Guam's jungles green and lush but eerily quiet.

activities to keep you busy when you're not diving. For nature lover, hikes into Guam's jungles can be fun. A few trails are well-marked and nothing in the way of plant or animal life is dangerous. There is a mountain biking trail along the upper Harmon Clif-fline. Sea kayaking is becoming popular and tours and trips along Guam's largely undeveloped southern coastline provide a nice look at Guam's geologic, historic and natural history.

A child paddles a bamboo canoe on the Talofofo River.

Sella Bay The overlook to this scenic bay is marked with a large sign off Highway 2 out of Agat. It is just the start of a trail that winds through the hills and grassy swordgrass plains to the valley below. Tall coconut trees in the river valleys and along the beach add a splash of green even during dry season.

Heading down the trail, a small wooden bridge leads over a part of the Sella River and into rolling, rocky country. The trail then goes through a beautiful jungle and runs parallel to the Sella River. Hermit crabs and Guam toads will scatter from the path as hikers wind around large coconut trees. This cool walk then opens up to Sella Bay.

The nicest snorkeling spots are away from the river outflows, where the runoff silt doesn't bother coral growth. The hike down usually takes about 30 minutes. On the way back it is all uphill, so allow an hour for rest and water stops. Bring plenty of water to drink.

Ypao Beach Park This large public beach along the southwest side of Tumon Bay was once the location of an ancient Chamorro village and in the late 1800s was the site of a penal and leper colony.

The park has playground equipment, picnic facilities and an expansive beachfront with white sand and turquoise waters. It's not only a popular weekend place for local families but it's also a well-used venue for festivals and other celebrations.

Gun Beach This beach is a third of a mile down the washed-out, but generally passable coral road that goes by the Hotel Nikko. It's named for the rusted Japanese gun that is half-hidden in jungle growth at the foot of the northside cliff.

The sand at Gun Beach is quite fascinating as it is largely comprised of tiny orange grains with little star-shaped points. Known as star sand, it's actually the calcium carbonate shells of a common protozoan found on Guam's reefs.

South Pacific Memorial Park A memorial site for those who died during WWII, the main monument here is a 15-ft abstract sculpture of large white hands folded in prayer, surrounded by personalized memorial plaques in Japanese script. A small chapel called the Queen of Peace is staffed by Japanese priests and nuns.

Steps lead down the hill from the monument to four caves, which served as the last Japanese Army command post. The caves are surrounded by a bamboo forest that creaks in the wind and is spooky enough to conjure up images of restless spirits.

The park, on Route 1 in Yigo, is open from 8 am to 5 pm daily.

War in the Pacific National Historical Park With a visitor center and WWII museum in Asan, the center's main displays combine period photos and military paraphernalia to give an engaging chronological history of Guam during the war years.

The center is open from 9 am to 5 pm Monday to Friday and from 10 am to 5 pm on weekends. Admission is free, as are brochures that map out the various battle sites around Guam.

Umatac Umatac is an unspoiled, friendly village, steeped in history. Magellan's 1521 landing in Umatac Bay is celebrated in the village each March with four days of activities, including a re-enactment of the event. A tall concrete monument to Magellan stands in the village center.

The Spanish used Umatac Bay for more than 200 years as a major port of call for their galleons, though little remains of the four forts that once protected the bay.

On your way out of town you'll see the decorative Umatac Bridge with its spiral staircase towers that are intended to salute Guam's Chamorro–Spanish heritage.

Diving Safety

TIM ROCK

Two things conspire against the diver in Micronesia: incredible water clarity and strong currents. You will have to be alert for changing conditions and monitor your depth closely. Before every dive, consider the way you feel that particular day, your level of training, physical condition and water conditions at the site. Remember, it is no sin to abort a dive.

Pre-trip Preparation

Generally, divers are most comfortable using their own gear, but as far as diving equipment goes, you can show up with nothing and leave Guam with just about every gadget known to diving. Due to an active local diving population, many stores are fully stocked with the top brand names at competitive prices. Replacing equipment or buying new gear is more difficult on Rota and Yap, as stock availability fluctuates and is not always dependable.

Learning to Dive

All levels of instruction are available on Guam, from snorkeling and basic open water to instructorship. PADI , NAUI and IANTD are the major training organizations. PADI courses are also available on Yap and Rota.

Technical diving is becoming quite popular on Guam and many shops offer mixed gas fills. Guam's unique terrain and various walls, wrecks, caves and drop-offs are perfect for

Diving and Flying

Most divers to Guam, Rota and Yap get there by plane. While it's fine to dive soon *after* flying, it's important to remember that your last dive should be completed at least 12 hours (some experts advise 24 hours) *before* your flight, to minimize the risk of residual nitrogen in the blood that can cause decompression injury.

learning advanced techniques. Check out the **Diving Services** listing (pg. 139) to find out more about dive courses offered by individual operations.

Medical

Guam has one permanent fully-staffed recompression chamber, run by the U.S. Navy on the COMNAVMARIANAS naval base. The chamber is operational 24-hours a day and can be reached at ☎ 671-339-7143 or ☎ 720-0342 in case of diving emergencies.

Guam has two hospitals, one military and one civilian, both staffed with physicians highly trained in diving accidents and medicine. Full medical services are also available through a number of well-staffed private clinics. Guam Memorial Hospital is at 850 Gov. Carlos Camacho Rd., Tamuning, ☎ 671-647-2330, Fax: 671-649-5508

On Yap, the state government operates a 150-bed hospital that is well stocked and professionally staffed. Intensive care, treatment for recompression and other serious injuries must be conducted off island. Med-a-Vac services are available to Guam or Manila.

DAN

Divers Alert Network (DAN) is an international membership association of individuals and organizations sharing a common interest in diving and safety. It operates a 24-hour diving emergency hotline, ☎ 919-684-8111 or 919-684-4DAN (-4326), which accepts collect calls in a dive emergency. DAN does not directly provide medical care; however, it does provide advice on early treatment, evacuation and hyperbaric treatment of diving-related injuries. Divers should contact DAN for assistance as soon as a diving emergency is suspected. DAN membership is reasonably priced and includes DAN TravelAssist, a membership benefit, which covers medical air evacuation from anywhere in the world for any illness or injury. For a small additional fee, divers can get secondary insurance coverage for decompression illness. For membership questions call ☎ 800-446-2671 in the U.S. or 919-684-2948 elsewhere.

Pisces Rating System for Dives & Divers

The dive sites in this book are rated according to the following diver skill level rating system. These are not absolute ratings but apply to divers at a particular time, diving at a particular place. For instance, someone unfamiliar with prevailing conditions might be considered a novice diver at one dive area, but an intermediate diver at another, more familiar location.

Novice: A novice diver generally fits the following profile:
◆ basic scuba certification from an internationally recognized certifying agency
◆ dives infrequently (less than one trip a year)
◆ logged fewer than 25 total dives
◆ dives no deeper than 18 meters (60 ft)
◆ little or no experience diving in similar waters and conditions
* A novice diver should be accompanied by an instructor or divemaster on all dives

Intermediate: An intermediate diver generally fits the following profile:
◆ may have participated in some form of continuing diver education
◆ logged between 25 and 100 dives
◆ dives no deeper than 40 meters (130 ft)
◆ has been diving within the last six months in similar waters and conditions

Advanced: An advanced diver generally fits the following profile:
◆ advanced certification
◆ has been diving for more than 2 years; logged over 100 dives
◆ has been diving within the last six months in similar waters and conditions

Regardless of skill level, you should be in good physical condition and know your limitations. If you are uncertain as to which category you fit, ask the advice of a local dive instructor. He or she is best qualified to assess your abilities based on the prevailing dive conditions at any given site. Ultimately you must decide if you are capable of making a particular dive, depending on your level of training, recent experience, and physical condition, as well as water conditions at the site. Remember that water conditions can change at any time, even during a dive.

Dive Site Icons

The symbols at the beginning of the dive site descriptions provide a quick summary of some of the following conditions present at the site:

 Good snorkeling or free diving site

 Cave or caverns. Only experienced cave divers should explore inner cave areas.

 Drift dive

 Deep dive. The best parts of the dive occur in water deeper than 90 feet (27 meters).

 Vertical wall or drop-off

 Strong surge likely

 Poor or limited visibility possible

 Strong currents likely

 Marine Preserve. Special regulations apply in this area

 Remains or partial remains of a shipwreck can be seen at this site.

Diving in Guam

TIM ROCK

With an active local diving community and a great variety of dive sites, Guam has grown into a popular dive destination for Japanese tourists, and is gaining in popularity with other Asian and stateside divers.

Divers visiting Guam will want to see the WWII shipwrecks and experience the novelty dives like the Blue Hole or The Crevice, known for their water clarity. Daily charters to popular sites are available through the local dive shops.

The best way to approach the reefs is by boat. This is safer and increases the likelihood of seeing fish and other sea creatures. The surf on Guam can be tricky and unpredictable. Even divers used to a surf entry could be in for a surprise on Guam, where water crosses a broad reef flat before breaking. Undercurrents and rips in the cuts are strong when the surf is up and tides are changing.

Apra Harbor dives are all done on hard coral reefs or shipwrecks. Most sites are just a short ride from the docks and the well-protected harbor is diveable year round. Many reefs cascade down, gently sloping to 90 ft (27 meters) or deeper. The shipwrecks range in depths from 60 to 120 ft (18 to 37 meters). Outer reefs provide variety, ranging from deep drop-offs to coral flats.

Due to rapid development, Guam sometimes

Wreck Diving

Wreck diving can be safe and fascinating. Penetration of shipwrecks, however, is a skilled specialty and should not be attempted without proper training. Wrecks are often unstable; they can be silty, deep and disorienting. Use an experienced guide to view wrecks and the amazing coral communities that have developed on them.

has a siltation problem on its reefs. Many of the offshore reefs escape this blight, however, and provide homes to fish, sea anemones and hard and soft corals.

Divers used to Caribbean diving will feel at home on Guam dive boats as divemasters are present and keep groups small, usually 4 to 6 divers per divemaster. Operators cater mainly to Japanese tourists, so Guam diving can easily become a cross-cultural experience. A number of divemasters and instructors work through the local shops to provide service on a one-to-one basis by using their private boats. If you have specific sites in mind or want to keep your group small, ask the local shops about a private charter.

The larger charter boats also offer early morning single-tank dives and afternoon/evening dives that include on-deck barbecues and a night dive. Night diving on Guam is very good; a lot of unusual invertebrates that hide in the hard corals during the day, but come out to feed at night.

Snorkeling in Guam, Rota & Yap

Snorkeling in the islands of the Western Pacific can be just as enjoyable as scuba diving. For those not experienced with the sea, snorkeling is the best introduction to the coral reef and its many creatures. The colors, shapes and movements of the ocean create an indelible impression of awe; the experience often inspires snorkelers to become divers and never ceases to draw reef-lovers back to the sea, time after time.

On Guam, Yap and Rota, the inner reef and outer reef are separated by a barrier reef flat in most cases. Snorkeling on either side of these flats can be quite rewarding.

The shallow inner lagoons shelter lots of brightly colored tropical fish. The reflective sand in the inner lagoon is illuminated by the strong tropical sun and adds to the brilliance of this incredible world. Look for small juvenile fish among the coral heads, branching corals and sea grasses.

Over the reef, look for the grander coral formations, larger schools and bigger fish. Sea anemones like to sit within the coral gardens, providing havens for frisky clownfish. Snorkeling along the drop-offs of these islands can create a true sense of wonder as the blue abyss

TIM ROCK

Many popular dives serve as colorful snorkeling sites.

comes into view below. Here, the sun rays dance through the water. Look for pelagic fish in the deeper water and for manta rays along the drop-offs in Yap's channels.

In general, water for snorkeling will be clearest and safest at slack high tide. Also, snorkeling away from runoff areas will mean better visibility. Always ask about prevailing currents and tidal changes and make sure someone knows where you are and when you expect to return. The tropical sun can be intense, so wear a dive skin, a T-shirt and/or waterproof sunscreen when snorkeling.

Agat Bay Dive Sites

Agat Bay is a large expanse of water running parallel to and north of Agat village. You won't find an abundance of big coral heads, but rather a scattered system of patch reefs, sandy flats and channels. There are a number of popular dive sites in the bay, but much of the seascape here is still unexplored. Patient divers, amateur biologists and macrophotographers will enjoy this area because the seemingly barren reaches are actually alive with a large variety of plants and animals.

Similarly, a swim to some of the mid-depth areas south of the Namo River outfall can reveal an active ocean. There you'll see a scattering of coral heads mostly overgrown with encrusting sponges, algae, ascidians and hydroids. Tree worms dot many corals in an array of colors from sky blue to maroon and cream. They share their homes with tiny shrimp whose pincers and antennae peek out of tiny holes. Palm-size sea stars also make the flats home. They range in color from military green to peppermint striped reds and whites. Nudibranchs are also found in great diversity here.

Guam's Blue Hole.

The sandy bottom attracts large, disc-like rays with their mottled skin. They bury themselves in the sand much like the southern stingrays of the Bahamas. Hawksbill turtles swim through here and an occasional eagle ray my glide by, adding excitement to a dive.

While Agat Bay diving isn't for everyone, it is far from boring for those who know what they want to see and have the patience to look for it. Even when the minute targets don't pan out, there is always a chance of being swooped by a manta ray or escorted back to shore by spinner dolphins.

Agat Bay Dive Sites

Agat Bay Dive Sites	Good Snorkeling	Novice	Intermediate	Advanced
Blue Hole			✓	✓
Barracuda Rock	✓	✓	✓	✓
3 The Crevice			✓	✓
4 Shark Pit			✓	✓
5 Eel Gardens			✓	✓
6 Rizal Coral Heads	✓	✓	✓	✓
7 Hap's Reef	✓	✓	✓	✓
8 Gaan Point		✓	✓	✓
9 The Amtrac		✓	✓	✓
10 Coral Gardens	✓	✓	✓	✓
11 Pete's Reef			✓	✓

1 Blue Hole

Guam's Blue Hole is one of the island's finest variety dives. Toward the tip of the Orote Peninsula, the hole can usually be seen from the land directly in front of an A-marker. With the photogenic hole in the background, this site is a popular spot for everything from movie making to weddings and military re-enlistments.

The hole itself is basically a long, perpendicular shaft that starts at the top of a sloping reef flat in about 60 ft. The shaft itself extends down to about 300 ft, but at 130 ft a large window opens to the outer wall, allowing the diver to exit and ascend after a free fall through the shaft.

As the Blue Hole faces the open ocean, it is not unusual to see large fish like bar-

Location: Orote Peninsula
Depth Range: 60-130 ft (18-40 meters)
Access: Boat
Expertise Rating: Intermediate

racuda and dogtooth tuna. Eagle rays glide along the reef top and on rare occasions dolphins and pilot whales join boats traveling to the hole.

The Blue Hole is located away from runoff areas and visibility normally exceeds 100 ft. A Blue Hole dive needs to

Floating in the azure abyss of the Blue Hole.

be well-planned as it is on the deeper spectrum of sport diving. The top of the hole is at 60 ft. Once you get over the edge, the free fall begins. Many divers like to assume the role of skydiver and slow drift down to the window. This is indeed fun, but there is a lot to see along the way.

At 80 ft, a large crevice is home to many soldierfish. Orienting themselves to the bottom, many swim upside down in the recesses of the hole. At 100 ft, crimson sea whips and small fans along the northern wall make for colorful photographs. At night, the rare flashlight fish comes out and brightens the water. Light is biochemically generated in a sac under each eye, sending flickers of light into the black water. When active, the school resembles a group of fireflies.

2 Barracuda Rock

Location: Orote Peninsula
Depth Range: 15-60 ft (5-18 meters)
Access: Boat
Expertise Rating: Novice

This is a good spot for a shallow second dive. It is a fun place to poke around the small cave in the cliffline or tunnel in the big boulders. A colony of noddies occupies the big rock that marks this site. They will fly over approaching boats at first, but then settle down almost camouflaged on the volcanic boulder.

A small cave in the cliffline is home to a school of glassy copper sweepers. The cave isn't deep, nor does it go back very far, but there are stalactites that hang down, so be careful not to hit your head, especially if you are free diving inside the cave.

Outside the cave, to the right as you face the cliffline, is a tunnel that also has sweepers and bigeyes hiding in its recesses.

Other fish swim through and turtles have been known to sleep here at night.

The big boulders in the clear water at 30 to 60 ft are home to a variety of fish from juvenile Napoleon wrasse to regal angelfish. After dark, nocturnal fish like lionfish, are joined by starfish, crabs and other invertebrates coming out to forage.

TIM ROCK

The fish population around Barracuda Rock bursts with color and variety.

3 The Crevice

This deep dive along the Orote Peninsula is pretty but not overly endowed with marine life. You'll find golden gorgonian fans deep in the crevice and some soft corals. Lace corals fill some of the smaller fissures. The thrill of this dive is the chance encounter with some big creature from the open sea. Although not frequently encountered, sailfish and whale sharks have been reported here as have eagle rays and mantas. Deep at The Crevice's bottom, sharks can occasionally be seen resting under ledges.

The outer wall can also provide some wonderful surprises. Drift dives from The

Location: Orote Peninsula
Depth Range: 60-130 ft (18-40 meters)
Access: Boat
Expertise Rating: Advanced

Crevice to the Blue Hole are popular when currents are right.

The upper sand flats are used as decompression stops, although none of the reeftop is really shallow. Decompression stops should be taken on the mooring buoy lines situated at The Crevice.

4 Shark Pit

A huge rock rises to within 15 ft of the surface at the Shark Pit. Golden gorgonian sea fans grow in the cracks in the bottom recesses of the rock, where you'll find copper sweepers and bigeyes. Lionfish are found around the front of the boulder.

Location: Orote Peninsula, Tantapalo Point

Depth Range: 15-130 ft (5-40 meters)

Access: Boat

Expertise Rating: Intermediate

The entire area was a military dumpsite for years and very big sharks would congregate around the edge of the cliff looking for garbage to scavenge. Dumping has now ceased and seeing a shark here is a rarity, but old mess hall trays and all kinds of other military refuse still litter the bottom. Remnants of amtracs (amphibious tractors) and bulldozers are strewn about the area.

TIM ROCK

In the past, the Shark Pit was a major dumping ground for military ordnance.

5 Eel Gardens

Garden eels live in groups in the sand. They feed on passing plankton by partially hovering above their burrows, but quickly retreat without a sign or sound if they hear or see divers approach. So diving the Eel Gardens requires a kind and gentle approach to diving. Approach slowly. When you spot them, breath minimally so your bubbles don't spook them.

Location: Rizal Bay
Depth Range: 45-120 ft (14-36 meters)
Access: Boat
Expertise Rating: Intermediate

This site starts shallow along a huge sand wash that flows down into deep water off Rizal Bay. Triggerfish swim in the upper waters of this gradual drop-off. A couple of old cables lead you down into a large sandy plain. Once there, move slowly and look for movement on the sea floor.

The area around this flat features some beautiful sea anemones. Other fish and invertebrates, like pincushion starfish, entertain as well. This is a deep dive, even though it may not seem like it, so keep careful track of time and depth.

Pincushion starfish on the flats at Eel Gardens.

Approach slowly or the garden eels will pop back into the sand.

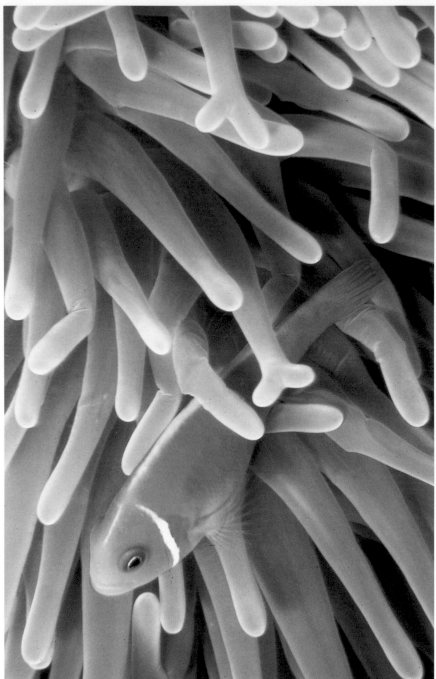

Skunk clownfish frolic in the flowing fingers of giant sea anemones.

6 Rizal Coral Heads

The coral heads at the north end of Rizal Beach make a great shallow second dive or snorkel. On a sunny day, the shallow coral reflects the sun, providing an excellent backdrop for photography or just a long, exploratory dive.

On some of the coral heads, you'll find anemone schools with lots of clownfish. This spot is great for the macrophotographer or videographer wanting to capture the playful antics of these fish.

The sandy patches between the heads are home to sea cucumbers and starfish. Also, watch the goby and the blind shrimp work together, while the goby acts as guardian for the ever-active, hole-clearing shrimp.

Location: Rizal Bay
Depth Range: 10-40 ft (3-12 meters)
Access: Boat
Expertise Rating: Novice

This site is not dived very much and can be reached from shore, but it is a more relaxing dive if approached by boat. Take some time to poke around in the many cracks found at the base of the coral head for invertebrates, such as Christmas tree worms.

7 Hap's Reef

Soldierfish are common at Hap's.

Location: Agat Bay
Depth Range: 20-60 ft (6-18 meters)
Access: Boat
Expertise Rating: Novice

Hap's Reef is one of Guam's unique undersea attractions. A loaf-shaped reef north of Gaan Point, it was developed by Guam tour operators and photo-minded divers.

Hap's has been featured in Japanese television specials and prominent dive/travel magazines.

In the past, divers hand-fed a variety of Pacific tropical fish here and, as it is in the open ocean in Agat Bay, a good variety of fish reside here.

However, these days divers are becoming more sensitive to local wildlife

TIM ROCK

Moray eels hide in the holes at Hap's Reef.

and over the years a sort of unspoken code has emerged regarding Hap's. Local fisherman rarely fish here anymore and moorings have been established in recent years.

TIM ROCK

Moongazers hover above the coral.

In the early '80s, the reef was wracked by dynamite blasts and spearfishing, which indiscriminately killed a lot of fish and coral. Heavy use by divers and an attack by the crown-of-thorns starfish has left the coral not as healthy as it once was.

But nonetheless, a dive on Hap's is far from disappointing. The swirl of reef tropicals is quite breathtaking to even the most jaded diver. Hap's appears to being steadily gaining in fish abundance. In addition, numerous sea anemones have been planted, producing an array of curious clownfish that happily pose for underwater photographers. Hap's is well worth the effort of a leisurely visit.

8 Gaan Point

Location: Agat Bay
Depth Range: 15-60 ft (5-18 meters)
Access: Boat or Beach
Expertise Rating: Novice

The Gaan Point site is full of large coral heads and a variety of sea anemones. The area is sometimes exposed to sewage outfall during high runoff, so it is best to dive here when it hasn't rained for a couple of days. That said, beach divers can follow a sandy channel out to the left of the point, which has a series of mini-atolls surrounded by sea grasses. There is an old Japanese boat in this channel, often attracting fish that hover inside the upside-down hull.

The swim out follows a mini-wall on one side and a channel with coral heads on the other. Occasionally, a large barracuda comes into this channel. Look for invertebrate life in the coral heads, including tiny burrowing shrimp.

The channel opens to a broad sandy area with many large coral heads. The wall also continues to the right and large fish have made homes in the wave-washed crevices. Each coral head has something unique to offer. One extends from the bottom at 45 ft up to 25 ft, covered with leather coral that attracts sergeant majors and other damsels. Take time to look around closely. This was a major WWII invasion site as well and, even now, an occasional helmet or gas mask gets uncovered by shifting sands.

TIM ROCK

A mini wall of soft leather corals and anemones at the historic Gaan Point.

TIM ROCK

The Amtrac was left behind after U.S. forces invaded Guam. The glass windows are still intact.

9 The Amtrac

The Amtrac (amphibious tractor) was part of the U.S. invasion force that stormed the island in 1944. It is one of many amtracs that once rested on the bottom of Agat Bay. A few years ago, a salvage company was contracted by the military to recover the vehicles. Most have been removed, but this amtrac was left behind. There is also a tank turret and tracks to the north.

Location: Gaan Point, Agat Bay
Typical Depth: 50 ft (15 meters)
Access: Boat
Expertise Rating: Novice

The swim to The Amtrac can be a long one and many people prefer to snorkel out, diving on the way back to conserve air. It is not difficult to find, however, as it rests on white sand off the point.

A little compass navigation is about all that is needed to find this war relic. The diver should go to the end of the Gaan Point jetty and look for a large coral head in the middle of the south channel. It sits almost parallel with the end of the pipeline.

The trip to The Amtrac is at 20 to 30 ft, opening to a 50 foot bottom, so air consumption should not be too much of a problem for a diver in good condition.

10 Coral Gardens

Location: Inner Anae Island
Depth Range: 10-50 ft (3-15 meters)
Access: Boat
Expertise Rating: Novice

Guam's varied reef structures allow divers to explore a number of different offshore formations. The most popular reefs are accessible, somewhat shallow and easy to reach. The Coral Gardens fit the bill.

Boat diving is recommended and the launch site at the north end of Nimitz Beach is available. There is also a beach launch convenient for inflatable and small craft owners at the southern end of the park. The Agat Marina is also very close and has slips and a launching ramp.

The Coral Gardens are in the large channel that flows past Anae Island into Facpi Bay. You know you're close when you spot the rocks that break the surface near the east shore of Anae. Some corals rise very close to the surface at low tide, so be careful.

The beauty of diving the Gardens comes from the great variety of sites within the area. Divers should make a number of trips here to explore the various formations in the channel. Close to the island, huge coral pillars rise as high as 25 ft. An entire dive can be made exploring the various pinnacles and their accompanying sea life.

At the edge of the Gardens in 55 ft, the sandy sea floor is interspersed with coral and algae-encrusted mounds. Starfish, moray eels and snoozing whitetip sharks are common here. Soldierfish and squirrelfish also hide under the ledges of these coral hills.

Many dives can be made on these reefs and you can experience new sea life each time. Be careful here during the trade wind months when small, stinging man-o-wars sometimes invade the area. Check the water before plunging.

Spinner dolphins sometimes come in and will play in the wake of the boat.

The odd-looking juvenile dragon wrasse.

A linkia starfish drapes itself over the coral.

This is an added pleasure that, combined with a long dive, makes the Coral Gardens attractive. Also, there is topside cave on Anae Island and divers can climb up and take a land tour if desired.

11 Pete's Reef

This site was named for Guam's veteran undersea explorer Pete Peterson, who established it as a dive site. This dive presents a nice mix of small caves, coral heads and sandy patches that provide homes for a variety of marine life.

Location: Facpi Bay
Depth Range: 20-80 ft (6-24 meters)
Access: Boat
Expertise Rating: Intermediate

Many small tunnels and nooks sit at 50 ft and can be safely passed through. Starfish, other invertebrates and an occasional eel like to inhabit the inside of these maze-like holes. Look under the ledges at Pete's and you'll usually find a whitetip shark. The reef is open to the sea and sometimes a pelagic fish will come in here. Dolphins use this bay to rest and mate.

Anemones decorate the corals and some in the sand are well worth photographing, including the unusual sand anemone, which hosts variety of damsel clownfish.

Pete's is also a good night dive as crustaceans like anemone crabs and planktonic creatures, form a clusters of frenzied action around a video light or strong dive light.

TIM ROCK

Spinner dolphins rest and mate in Facpi Bay.

Southern Coast Dive Sites

Guam's coast Highway 2 heads south out of Agat village into the beautiful hills of Guam. The bays and reefs of southern Guam are among the most popular on the island. The western side is calm and well-protected most of the year and features a deep barrier reef with peninsular drop-offs, attracting all levels of diver. Minimal diving takes place on the eastern side and usually only in the summer months.

Southern coast dive sites feature colorful walls off the barrier reef and deep caves.

Villages such as Umatac and Inarajan give visitors a glimpse of a more rural Guam, whose character remains relatively unaffected by tourism. The Southern end of the island presents a picturesque mix of volcanic hills and valleys, threaded together by numerous rivers, waterfalls and protected bays.

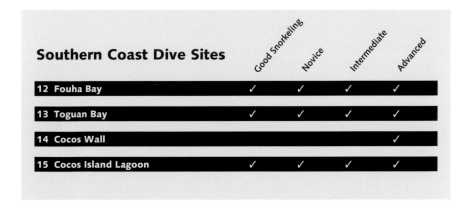

Southern Coast Dive Sites	Good Snorkeling	Novice	Intermediate	Advanced
12 Fouha Bay	✓	✓	✓	✓
13 Toguan Bay	✓	✓	✓	✓
14 Cocos Wall				✓
15 Cocos Island Lagoon	✓	✓	✓	✓

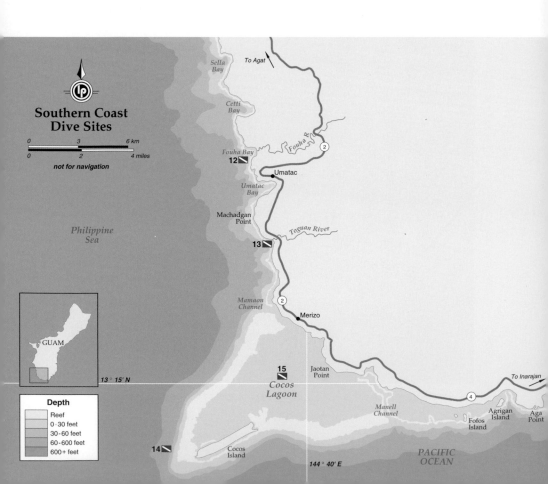

12 Fouha Bay

Not too many folks stop at Fouha. It is shallow and often overlooked, but some small caves and crevices are large enough to be entered. Also interesting is the mysterious airplane wreckage, which speculators say may be the remnants of a WWII plane shot down during a Guam fighter plane battle.

Location: North of Umatac
Depth Range: 3-30 ft (1-9 meters)
Access: Boat
Expertise Rating: Novice

Just north of Umatac Bay, Fouha is, at times, home to some of the spinner dolphins that stay in Guam's sheltered bays to rest or sleep. The bottom is somewhat silty and covered with natural debris, as it is a spillway for the Fouha River that flows down from Guam's rolling hills.

Facing the shore from the sea, the left side of the bay has some small caves that make nice sites for photography when the sun is high. Sun shafts streak through the cracks in the top of this honeycombed reef and create great dances of light inside the caverns.

Schools of small sweepers make these caves home and flash in and out of sight when a dive light is shined their way.

STEPHANIE BRENDL

Juvenile sweepers in the caves at Fouha Bay.

13 Toguan Bay

This is an area that is calm most of the year except when there is a southern swell. Park just off the road by the village sign at the bridge, suit up and wade across the reef flat. Enter the water at the shelf where the small Toguan River empties into the sea and swim left to see caves, holes and scattered coral heads.

Location: Mouth of Toguan River

Depth Range: 10-60 (3-18 meters)

Access: Beach or Boat

Expertise Rating: Novice

Numerous canyons feature schools of bream and goatfish. Weaving in and out of the caverns can be fun, but don't penetrate too far as silt can get kicked up, making for an uncomfortable exit if you meet a dead end.

There is a mini-wall of healthy coral and a big coral head with a large anemone and other invertebrate life farther south. Explore the sandy outer reaches and look for mottled rays, shells and an occasional shark. Spinner dolphins also come into this area and occasionally their calls can be heard. They rarely approach divers however, as they seem to dislike bubbles.

This can be a good night dive with cowries and other shell life coming out of the caves to feed.

The Dolphins

Guam's coastal waters home to pods of spinner dolphins *(Stinella longirostris)*, which are attracted to the island's shallow bays. Easily identified by their long, slender bodies and a long thin snout or beak, the spinner's flippers and flukes are large and pointed. Their topside is medium-to-dark gray, while the underbelly is quite pale. The larger dolphins can reach 7 ft in length and weigh up to 200 pounds. They are known to live for 25 to 30 years.

Spinner dolphins are warm-blooded social creatures that travel in large schools. Lucky locals have established a rapport with the animals and even enjoy snorkeling sessions with them in the southern end of Guam. The dolphins attain at speeds of up to 45 mph, so if they slow down to play with you, it is because they want to. It is this fact, among others, that make a dolphin encounter on Guam a special experience.

Unlike some Caribbean destinations, there are no trained dolphins on Guam to swim with. All dolphin encounters are in-the-wild happenings.

TIM ROCK

TIM ROCK

Exploring caves with a dive light will bring out the color of the walls and help you navigate.

14 Cocos Wall

Cocos Island sits at Guam's southernmost tip and is swept by almost constant currents as the Pacific Ocean and the Philippine Sea meet and sweep south to other reefs and sea mounts.

Location: Outside Cocos Island
Depth Range: 40-130 ft (12-40 meters)
Access: Boat
Expertise Rating: Advanced

You might expect a lot of fish life here, but there isn't. The more fantastic sea life is at the deep end of the diving scale here. A wall—actually a strongly pitched slope— follows along the outer edge of Cocos Island and provides a glimpse at some beautiful sea life and an occasional pelagic fish. Look down and out for a glimpse at a big Napoleon wrasse or at a school of buffalo parrotfish, grazing on the corals like herds of undersea buffalo.

Sea whips are found along the wall, where the current varies, depending on the moon and the time of day. These gorgonian whips are a crimson red when illuminated by a strong light or underwater camera strobe. Look for jacks and schools of sharpnose barracuda that may come in out of curiosity.

A sea anemone closed-up at night.

15 Cocos Island Lagoon

Location: Southern barrier reef
Depth Range: 2-30 ft (1-9 meters)
Access: Beach or boat
Expertise Rating: Novice

The sandy flats and scattered coral heads inside the Cocos barrier reef in southern Guam offer fascinating snorkeling or diving for patient and curious divers. While not blessed with the more ornate formations found in Agat's Coral Gardens, this area is very much alive with marine life, especially from the smaller end of the animal world. The sea grasses growing inside the lagoon offer protection for a number of juvenile animals not fully prepared for the more competitive world of the coral reef. Everything from miniature octopus to young barracuda and skipjack thrive in this environment.

Small anemones wave from holes in scattered rocks and coral heads. Banded shrimp set up cleaning stations and sharp-eyed observers can also spot the translucent glass shrimp, virtually melting into the sandy terrain. Gently overturning rocks can reveal bristleworms in many sizes and pastel colors, file shells with their flowing tentacles and clinging shells full with a hermit crab or the original owner. The Bikini Island area, the small sand spit next to Cocos, is a good spot for finding these critters. The reef side of Bikini has stands of staghorn coral that protect blue chromis and anemone colonies with the one-stripe clownfish. There are also a lot of burrowing crabs in the area. If you are interested in a relaxing afternoon, try the shallows of Cocos Lagoon.

Sea whips on the Cocos Wall.

An aerial view of Cocos Island.

Northwest Coast Dive Sites

The reefs of northern Guam range from deep drop-offs to shallow bays, filled with colorful fish. The coral-filled inner lagoons are great for snorkelers, fish-watchers and macrophotographers.

The outer reefs from the Agana Boat Basin to Two Lover's Point slope into deep water or drop straight down. The cliffline sites here are washed by currents that keep the water clear and flushed. Humpback whales have been seen taking respite during annual migrations. Spinner dolphin families rest in the shallow bays and manta rays are frequently seen along the outer Tumon and Gun Beach reefs. Dogtooth tuna, mahi-mahi and blue marlin are among the seasonal pelagics that can be found in this doorway to the Philippine Sea.

These reefs are exposed to trade winds during part of the year and aren't dived as frequently as southern reefs. This makes exploration here even more exciting. Night diving is especially good as the many coral crevices harbor a plethora of nocturnal invertebrates. Diving is best here during the summer months when the sea is flat calm.

Northwest Coast Dive Sites	Good Snorkeling	Novice	Intermediate	Advanced
16 Piti Channel	✓	✓	✓	✓
17 Piti Bomb Holes	✓	✓	✓	✓
18 Fish Eye Marine Park	✓	✓	✓	✓
19 Asan Cut and Beach			✓	✓
20 Hospital Point		✓	✓	✓
21 Tumon Bay		✓	✓	✓
22 Gun Beach	✓		✓	✓
23 Shark's Hole	✓		✓	✓
24 Double Reef	✓	✓	✓	✓
25 The Pinnacle				✓

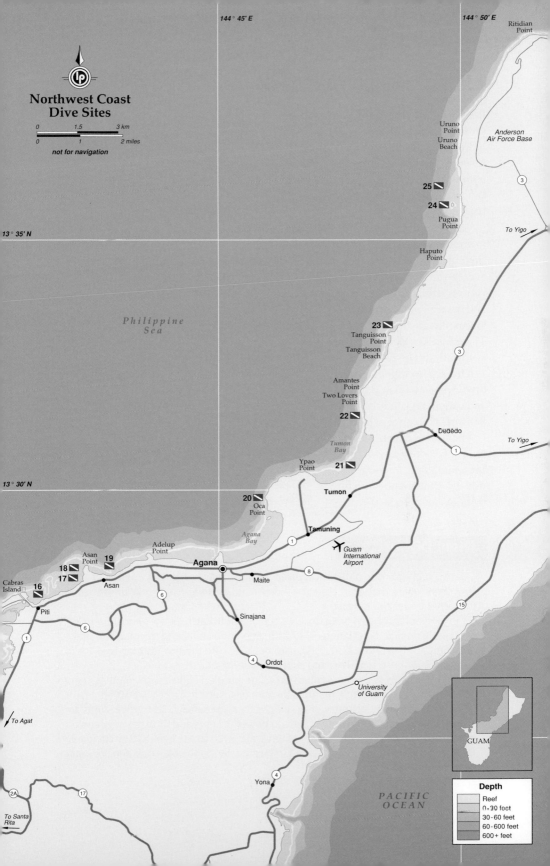

Northwest Coast
Dive Sites

0   1.5   3 km
0   1   2 miles

not for navigation

144° 45' E

144° 50' E

Ritidian
Point

Uruno
Point

Anderson
Air Force Base

Uruno
Beach

25

24   0

To Yigo

Pugua
Point

13° 35' N

Haputo
Point

3

*Philippine
Sea*

23

Tanguisson
Point

Tanguisson
Beach

3

Amantes
Point

Two Lovers
Point

22

Dededo

To Yigo

*Tumon
Bay*

1

Ypao
Point

21

Tumon

13° 30' N

20

Oca
Point

Tamuning

*Agana
Bay*

1

Guam
International
Airport

Adelup
Point

Agana

Maite

8

Asan
Point   **19**

18

17

6

Cabras
Island

16

Asan

Piti

6

Sinajana

1

15

6

4   Ordot

University
of Guam

To Agat

GUAM

2A

17

*PACIFIC
OCEAN*

4   Yona

To Santa
Rita

Depth

Reef

0-30 feet

30-60 feet

60-600 feet

600+ feet

16 Piti Channel

Piti Channel is often the first dive made for those learning to dive on Guam. It is used by instructors because it isn't too deep, still offers a good experience and its sandy bottom allows divers to practice new skills. But it shouldn't be dismissed as just a "beginner's dive."

Location: West of USO, Piti Village
Typical Depth: 30 ft (9 meters)
Access: Beach
Expertise Rating: Novice

This channel is great for the macrophotographer to shoot invertebrates like glass shrimp, hermit crabs, tree worms and even a rare seahorse. Scorpionfishes of various sizes, shapes and colors stay here and a rare lionfish with yellow marking lives in the rocks. These fishes are venomous, so keep your distance.

This is also a good night dive, when Spanish dancers and various brilliantly colored flatworms come out of hiding.

The channel entrance is said to be a favorite gathering site for manta rays at outgoing tide. Dive the channel mouth by boat, however, as the currents can become quite strong and sweep a diver out to sea. The inner channel current is rarely a problem.

Hermit crabs are excellent macrophotography subjects.

Night Diving

Guam is probably one of the most dived Pacific islands at night. A number of shallow shore dives that aren't great by day have an interesting mix of life when inspected under the dive light.

Photographers should bring close-up equipment to catch Guam's nocturnal invertebrates. Crinoids, pencil urchins, shrimp, anemone crabs and sleeping fish make easy prey for the photo buff. Take care not to startle the fish, as they may try to take off, injuring themselves and escaping your shot.

Piti Channel is known for colorful red and purple Spanish Dancers that come out at night. The Blue Hole features the rare flashlight fish at about 100 ft. Hap's is full of unusual invertebrates, including many nudibranchs. Some dive shops are trying plankton dives, where they turn on powerful lights and drop down into open ocean and see what kind of odd plankton is attracted to the light. Other creatures, like whale sharks or manta rays, can also be attracted to the plankton and are especially exciting to see at night.

17 Piti Bomb Holes

Piti's Bomb Holes are easily recognizable as you drive south on Marine Drive and enter the village of Piti. Located inside the reef, the holes take on a deep blue caste surrounded by varying shades of turquoise. They are as appealing to snorkel or dive in as they are to view from the land. They are not deep and the highly reflective white sand bottom makes for a colorful dive.

To reach the holes, one can wade or snorkel to the edge, depending on the tide. The northernmost hole is the largest and most popular with divers. The reef flat near the hole has a number of soft corals growing on it, along with a type of sea anemone that resembles soft coral but retracts quickly when approached. This animal can be toxic to humans and touching it should be avoided entirely.

The sand flats also produce another stinging creature, the cone shell. This animal is extremely toxic and should be

Location: Piti shoreline

Typical Depth: 35 ft (11 meters)

Access: Beach

Expertise Rating: Novice

Bomb Holes, or Not?

In reality, "bomb holes" were probably not caused by war. The term was adapted from local slang after Guam experienced heavy shelling during the American retaking of the island. But Richard Randall of the University of Guam Marine Lab says the holes are more likely collapsed caves that have filled with sea or sand. Guam's crust is honeycombed with many holes, caves and lava tubes, both above and below the surface.

The Piti Bomb Holes make for a colorful, relaxing dive or snorkel.

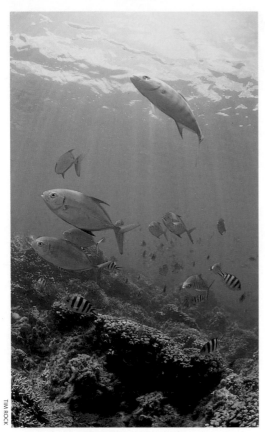

TIM ROCK

The holes are home to over 200 species of fish.

high tides. Take care when swimming out to negotiate the flow without tiring yourself before you get to the dive.

The soft corals end and the sandy slope leading into the hole takes over. The hole is about 35 ft deep and contains a number of large coral heads. In the nooks and crannies of the corals you'll find moray eels, octopi and lionfish.

Moorish idols and small butterflyfish are seen abundantly during the day. Pipefish skirt the top of the coral heads and needlefish skim the water overhead, swimming just below the surface and following the diver's bubbles.

In some areas, large concentrations of zoanthids (small disc-like creatures) are found in groupings like a multitude of toadstools.

The Bomb Holes can also be a nice spot for night diving. During a full moon, the white sand acts as a reflector so you can turn off your light and experience the surreal.

completely avoided. It has a poison barb it can actually fire like arrow.

Another danger to watch out for is the rip current that can run through the flats and make the going tough during some

In all, the Bomb Holes are good for snorkelers and beginning divers to sharpen skills. Even the "old pros" enjoy this site for a hassle-free, relaxing way to view the undersea world.

18 Fish Eye Marine Park

The recent addition of the Fish Eye Undersea Observatory into the largest bomb hole has given snorkelers and divers another site to explore. The observatory is a large structure that is connected to land by a long boardwalk. Inside, viewers stay perfectly dry while watching the fish.

Location: Piti Bay
Depth Range: 5-35 ft (1.5-11 meters)
Access: Beach
Expertise Rating: Novice

For those of us who prefer to get wet, the observatory is the most certain place to see lots of fish. A diver feeds fish for the public every hour. The facility has also transplanted some sea anemones, tridacna clams and small corals to sit in front of the windows. These can make good macro subjects.

Nearby, Seawalker Tours, an operation for non-divers to experience the sea, oper- ates from the pier in about 15 ft. Many fish gather here as well.

After the 1993 earthquake cracked and tumbled coral here, much work was done to keep the coral intact while the obser- vatory was being built. Fish and coral life around the observatory is varied. Sand anemones and other invertebrates, like crabs, can be seen through the observa- tory's immense viewing cylinder.

TIM ROCK

The undersea observatory can be visited by divers and snorkelers, or by non-divers via a walkway to the capsule.

TIM ROCK

Along with some corals and anemones, tridacna clams were transplanted to the area.

19 Asan Cut & Beach

Location: Asan Village shoreline

Depth Range 20-60 ft (6-18 meters)

Access: Beach

Expertise Rating: Intermediate

Asan Cut is located in front of Shelton's Music in Asan. A dive here can only be done under ideal conditions. The reef configuration makes it dangerous during times of even moderate surf. Currents and siltation—both factors here—can cause poor visibility.

July is one of the better times of the year to venture in here. Parking south of Shelton's Music puts you in close proximity with the shore. There are a few trees for shade—watch out for loose coconuts! Nearby is the War in the Pacific National Historical Park and Camel Rock.

The entry point is pretty obvious as the reef forms a "V" along the top of the reef flat. A moderate walk to the edge where the reef drops to about 20 ft, makes it easy to slide into the water. The Asan River empties onto the reef close by. The best visibility is to the south, but the remnants of a WWII amtrac lie to the north in 20 to 25 ft. Snorkel to it, make a short dive and then head for clearer water to the south.

Asan was an invasion site for American troops and many people lost their lives during fierce battle. At times divers will spot spent and live ammunition on the sand bottom and along the reef. The safest bet is to let it lie.

Near the shoreline there are schools of herbivorous fishes. The bottom is noted for having small tunicates, hydroids and other attached invertebrates.

A veined nudibranch along the shallow bottom at Asan.

TIM ROCK

TIM ROCK

Hard and soft corals compete for space on Guam's reefs.

20 Hospital Point

Hospital Point is a deep but beautiful dive off the Tamuning/Tumon cliffline, below Guam Memorial Hospital. The major attractions are the clear, blue water, a sloping drop-off punctuated with caves, sea fans, sea whips and the possibility of seeing large pelagic fish like tuna, barracuda, bumphead parrotfish and sharks. This deep area is infrequently dived so don't be surprised to hear about sightings of dolphins, sailfish, marlins or other large sea animals not usually seen along other parts of Guam's barrier reefs. A humpback whale

Location: Tamuning cliffline
Depth Range: 20-130 ft (6-40 meters)
Access: Boat
Expertise Rating: Intermediate

and calf were sighted along here once and the pair stayed close to shore for two days.

The dive is most conveniently done from the Agana Boat Basin. The cliffs drop sharply into the sea. They provide habitat for sea birds and coconut crabs. The drop-off isn't severe but it is pronounced. The best way to dive this site is as a drift dive. Currents here can be strong and tricky at times, non-existent at others. Just drop in and swim along the gradual drop-off starting at the deepest part of your dive and slowly move up.

The water here is extremely clear and it is easy to go beyond your planned depth, so keep an eye on your gauges and set a depth alarm if you have one. The sand bottom along the drop is probably 250 ft deep or more. It quickly falls to 600 then 1200 ft. Diving at about 100 ft will allow the diver to see sea fans and a variety of reef fish. Clown triggerfish appear here, along with schools of pyramid butterflyfish that like to congregate along the edges. Sea anemones are found at shallower depths.

As you swim up at the end of the dive for a safety decompression stop, notice the many cracks and crevices near the cliffline, home to scores of tiny baitfish and skipjacks. Moray eels live in the holes in the pocked corals. Beware of the surge if the seas or swells are up.

Gin-clear water makes fish watching easy.

21 Tumon Bay

Tumon Bay runs from the Reef Hotel to the Hilton International. The terrain within these azure waters includes shallow reef flats, patch coral, coral thickets and bright, white sand flats. Tumon Bay is the ideal place for the fish-watcher. An outdoor aquarium of sorts, Tumon has many of the area's most common marine tropicals in abundance. Probably the most popular dive or snorkeling site is at the bay's southern end at Ypao Beach.

This is one of the deeper areas within Tumon, purposely dredged for swimming. A lifeguard is on duty here and most of the time hazards like windsurfers and jet skiers are shooed away. This site is filled with branching staghorn corals, which provide shelter, food, breeding and spawning areas for other marine life. Toward the outer reef, brilliant blue chromis are abundant, feeding in groups just below the surface as their shiny silver sides reflect the sun's rays. When a snorkeler approaches too closely, they will form a tighter formation and dive for the safety of the staghorn thicket.

Other species including juvenile squirrelfish, tangs, butterflyfish, long-nosed filefish and the eel-like pipefish also use the staghorn branches for protection. The pipefish, by the way, is a close cousin of the seahorse. The male actually incubates the eggs in a ventral pouch until they hatch, just as seahorses do. Pipefishes are quite common on Tumon. A diverse eel population lives in the sandy reef flats. The honeycomb provides prime habitat for many species like the snowflake eel, spotted morays and the foul-tempered viper moray.

Tumon is a fine place for aspiring fish photographers who want to spend a long time underwater and for those who just like to look around at the sea.

Location: Tumon Bay
Depth Range: 5-15 ft (1.5-5 meters)
Access: Beach
Expertise Rating: Novice

Juvenile spotted cube trunkfish.

The ghost pipefish hides in coral branches.

22 Gun Beach

Gun Beach is one of Guam's most accessible dives and is a popular site for watching a great variety of fish and other large creatures. Manta rays and dolphins are seen here on occasion.

In front of the Nikko Hotel next to Fafai Beach, Gun Beach is named for the WWII Japanese shore gun found along the cliffline. Tumon was never invaded, so in all likelihood the gun was never fired in battle. The area was shelled by Americans, however.

Most people enter through the cable cut at Gun Beach, the easiest route when surf is low. A nasty rip forms here when water is high, however, which can make returning difficult, so keep this in mind.

There are nice coral formations in 25 to

Location: Gun Beach Cut
Depth Range: 20-120 ft (6-37 meters)
Access: Beach or Boat
Expertise Rating: Intermediate

50 ft to the south and large holes to the north. Sea anemones and crevalle jacks often come in to feed. Some fish feeding is done here, although it is not recommended as this is open ocean and you never know what will join your party. Sharks and large barracuda come through here occasionally.

TIM ROCK

Reclusive coral shrimps spend their lives hidden in the coral heads.

23 Shark's Hole

The name Shark's Hole sounds a little daunting, but this is a shallow dive that can be reached by boat or by a scenic walk along the beach north of Tanguisson. Despite the name, it is not known as a shark-spotting. Considered more of a snorkeling spot than a dive, it has an added bonus for hikers. In the jungle behind its beach is a freshwater swimming hole complete with a rope swing from a rock into the pool. Small fish live in this pool and tadpoles hatch here as well.

In the hole itself, healthy corals are fed by an exchange of water from cuts on both ends of the hole. It has been rated intermediate, as outgoing currents can be very strong. Only experienced snorkelers should venture near the mouth.

Location: North of Tanguisson Beach
Depth Range: 5-20 ft (1.5-6 meters)
Access: Beach
Expertise Rating: Intermediate

Parrotfish, chromis and healthy hard corals are found here and the sandy bottom is good for underwater photography. For those approaching from the sea, a dive along the outer slope may produce surprises. Manta rays live all along this upper coast and may appear here if luck is with you.

TIM ROCK

The Shark's Hole is a pool of crystal blue water just north of Tanguisson Beach.

24 Double Reef

The ride to Double Reef is sometimes as much fun as the diving when you get there. The normal plan of action is to make a day of it as the setting is tranquil and the underwater terrain quite scenic.

The Double Reef lies just offshore near Pugua Point. An old military dumpsite is probably what caused the large, green cliff to be treeless in front of the reef. It makes a good landmark. The break on the second reef is usually quite apparent. The fringing inner reef is near a small, sandy beach that is carved out of the cliffline. There is a cave here that can be snorkeled.

The reefs have a lot of variety, interspersed with sand flats. When seen from the air, the deep blue of the outer drop-off quickly blends into the various shades of turquoise for an extremely colorful picture. I have seen from a helicopter a large pod of spinner dolphins playing in this shallow oasis.

Double Reef offers good spots for anchoring in the protected water behind

Location: Northwest coast
Depth Range: 5-70 ft
  (1.5-21 meters)
Access: Boat Dive
Expertise Rating: Novice

the outer reef. There are large sand pits in about 30 ft. The surrounding coral is thick and many spots sport growth so competitive that different species have grown into and over one another.

Most Double Reef dives are at a safe sport diving depth, allowing for plenty of bottom time. An offshore current occasionally picks up along the deeper, less protected reefs and should be respected. Your compass is a good companion for getting around on long, exploratory dives.

If you're lucky, you just might see a pod of spinner dolphins swimming in the shallows.

TIM ROCK

A diver explores the coral variety.

25 The Pinnacle

The Pinnacle should be considered an advanced dive and those with proper training should try this spot. Located offshore of Double Reef, The Pinnacle starts very deep and falls off into blue water quickly. The anchor is set at 110 ft or deeper and the currents, especially at shallower depths, can be very strong.

Location: Offshore North Coast

Depth Range: 110-155 ft
   (34-47 meters)

Access: Boat

Expertise Rating: Advanced

The main attraction here is the pelagic life. There are regular reports of both whitetip and gray reef sharks, schooling skipjacks, schooling barracuda and tanguisson or Napoleon wrasse.

The critter most adventurers hope to see here is the hammerhead shark. Hammerheads are most often sighted around the Apra Harbor mouth and at The Pin-nacle. These solitary and large sharks don't normally come very close, but when they do their unusual head shape makes them hard to mistake for any other shark.

TIM ROCK

The Pinnacle stands out for pelagic life, such as these schooling jacks.

TIM ROCK

A diver checks out a giant yellow sea fan that grows like a tree on the coral mound.

Apra Harbor Dive Sites

Guam has a number of diveable shipwrecks and airplanes that were sunk during the battles of WWII. It was the first U.S. possession captured during that conflict as it was invaded shortly after Pearl Harbor was bombed. The retaking of Guam came three years later after the island was shelled heavily for weeks. Air battles grounded Japanese planes and invasion troops stormed much of the southern and central western coasts. Remnants of those battles, from bullets to bombs, are still found today in the hills by unsuspecting, and often alarmed, bulldozer operators.

Apra Harbor Dive Sites	Good Snorkeling	Novice	Intermediate	Advanced
26 Tokai Maru	✓		✓	✓
27 SMS Cormoran				✓
28 Kitsugawa Maru				✓
29 Family Beach	✓	✓	✓	✓
30 American Tanker		✓	✓	✓
31 Seabee Junkyard	✓	✓	✓	✓
32 Hidden Reef			✓	✓
33 Fingers Reef	✓	✓	✓	✓
34 Rock's Reef	✓	✓	✓	✓
35 GabGab Beach	✓	✓	✓	✓
36 GabGab II Reef	✓		✓	✓
37 Western Shoals	✓	✓	✓	✓
38 Dry Dock Reef		✓	✓	✓

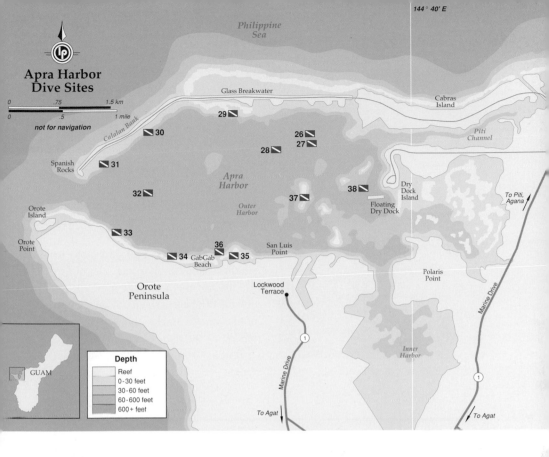

**Apra Harbor
Dive Sites**

Philippine
Sea

0   .75   1.5 km
0   .5   1 mile
not for navigation

Catalan Bank

Glass Breakwater

Cabras
Island

Piti
Channel

29

30

26
27

28

31

Apra
Harbor

Spanish
Rocks

38

Dry
Dock
Island

To Piti,
Agana

32

37

Floating
Dry Dock

Orote
Island

Outer
Harbor

Orote
Point

33

36

San Luis
Point

Polaris
Point

34   GabGab
Beach

35

Orote
Peninsula

Lockwood
Terrace

Marine Drive

Inner
Harbor

Marine Drive

GUAM

Depth
Reef
0-30 feet
30-60 feet
60-600 feet
600+ feet

1

To Agat

1

To Agat

26 *Tokai Maru*

Just east of the green marker buoy nearest the old seaplane ramp on the breakwater side of the harbor sits the *Tokai Maru*. It is a Japanese freighter sunk by a submarine torpedo attack during WWII. Oddly enough, it rests on another ship, the SMS *Cormoran*, which was scuttled during WWI. Thus, two victims of two different world wars rest touching in the harbor.

The *Tokai* is by far the more popular of the two as it is shallow enough to overswim in one dive. This ship sits at a list and can be somewhat disorienting. The bridge area is quite open and the combination of the maze of crossmembers and the slant of the ship have confused many a diver. There is not much to see inside except and old wash area with a tiled floor and

Location: Apra Harbor
Depth Range: 40-125 ft (12-38 meters)
Access: Boat
Expertise Rating: Intermediate

sink. The shafts of light coming through the doorways and beams make a nice scene, however.

The ship is not overgrown with coral, although it does have nice growth in some

TIM ROCK

The *Tokai*'s bow is dotted with tube corals.

spots. The bow has black and orange rope sponges growing along the rail and drain areas. This is a blessing because the ship is still recognizable and it is easy to get an idea what it looked like before it sunk.

The *Tokai* was a big freighter, about 500 ft long. The bow holds the scars of an explosion—watch for jagged metal. Her anchor chain is out and many cables and some winches are still on deck.

As it is a natural reef and close to another shallow harbor reef, a lot of fish live around the wreck. A good way to observe fish here is to go out on the end of the smoke stacks and watch them school. At the right time of day, a good deal of action takes place in the open water.

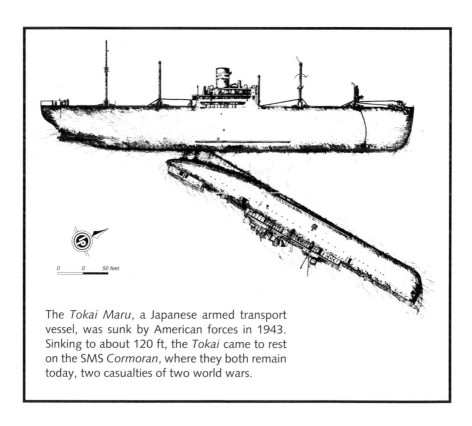

0   0   50 feet

The *Tokai Maru*, a Japanese armed transport vessel, was sunk by American forces in 1943. Sinking to about 120 ft, the *Tokai* came to rest on the SMS *Cormoran*, where they both remain today, two casualties of two world wars.

27 SMS *Cormoran*

The SMS *Cormoran* started claiming lives the day it sank. Seven crewmembers died after the ship's captain agreed to peacefully surrender the crew, but not give up the ship.

Location: Apra Harbor

Depth Range: 70-125 ft (21-38 meters)

Access: Boat

Expertise Rating: Advanced

On April 17, 1917, the first day of WWI, a U.S. Navy lieutenant was ordered to demand the ship's surrender. The German *Cormoran* had been in internment in Apra Harbor for a couple of years. The ship's crew were friendly with its American military counterparts, so the lieutenant left the *Cormoran* reluctantly when he heard the captain was unwilling to surrender the ship. As the lieutenant left in a skiff, the *Cormoran*'s captain gave orders to abandon ship.

Shortly after, an explosion—followed by smoke, flames and flying debris—ignited behind the bridge. The ship reportedly went down quickly, in less than 5 minutes after the explosion. Crew members were abandoning ship from the stern. It listed heavily to starboard, sitting horizontally, and sunk.

Seven crew members drowned before they could be picked up by a U.S. rescue ship. One was never found. The other six were buried in a little-used Naval cemetery that now sits in East Agana along the ocean side of Marine Drive.

In 1975 local author and diver Herb Ward, who wrote a book called *The Flight*

The *Cormoran* rests on its side and should only be explored by divers with proper wreck training.

of the Cormoran, also died while exploring the ship. In 1980, another diver was inside the ship when the compartment he was exploring silted over and he ran out of air trying to find his way out.

This ship is easily found as the *Tokai Maru* sits right on top of it. Just follow the marker chain down. Its anchor rests between the two ships. Or swim over the east side of the *Tokai* from about midships to the bow.

There isn't a lot to see as the holds are empty. Some fish make this ship their home and schooling jacks and fusiliers are often seen in the area. There is a lion claw bathtub and the wooden planking still remains on some floor areas. Most of the portholes have been removed. This ship is now protected; the removal of artifacts is against the law. Instructors have strung ropes in these ships and use them for wreck diving training.

The *Cormoran* is a great part of Guam and world history. Just remember that it is deep, silty and should be treated with a vast amount of respect.

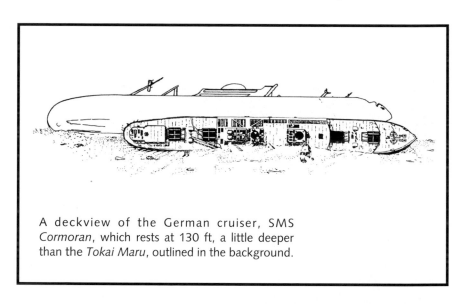

A deckview of the German cruiser, SMS *Cormoran*, which rests at 130 ft, a little deeper than the *Tokai Maru*, outlined in the background.

28 *Kitsugawa Maru*

Deep in the waters of Apra Harbor sits a mysterious and fascinating shipwreck. Once you've hooked the *Kitsugawa*, which can be a trick in itself, you play the channel visibility gamble. On those rare days of great visibility, what's left of the entire ship can come into view at about 50 ft. On the more usual days, visibility will be closer to 50 ft or less. This is still no problem as the ship is interesting to overswim.

Location: Apra Harbor
Depth Range: 60-140 ft (18-43 meters)
Access: Boat
Expertise Rating: Advanced

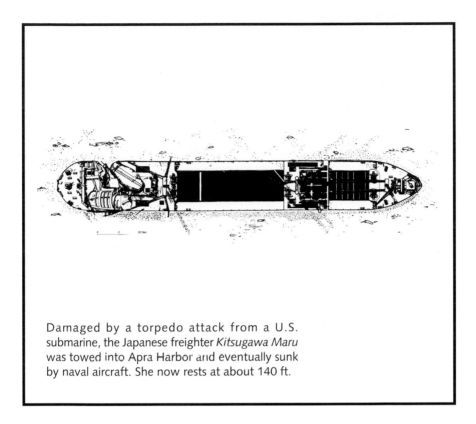

Damaged by a torpedo attack from a U.S. submarine, the Japanese freighter *Kitsugawa Maru* was towed into Apra Harbor and eventually sunk by naval aircraft. She now rests at about 140 ft.

Penetration is not recommended unless a well-thought plan has been devised. This ship is deep and the tables must be completely and conservatively respected here.

The stern is mangled. Air strike records indicate six definite hits to the midships. The report says pilots did not see any damage at first, but on a later strike the ship was reported sunk. It is guessed that damage was extensive enough to make her list so the cool sea water hit the hot boilers. The resulting explosion destroyed the stern.

The front mast and a cargo boom are still intact on the *Kitsugawa*. These are covered with encrusting corals and make a spectacular sight on a night dive. Some of the lines leading to the upper structures are still intact also.

Most divers like to visit the bowgun, which has managed to elude salvagers. The ammunition in the boxes in back of the gun is live and very, very unstable. It should be left alone. An octopus sometimes lives in one of the empty ammunition holes. At the right time of day the gun can be a fine photographic prop. A shot of the mast and perhaps a diver in the background with the gun in the fore is an enticing image. The bowgun is at around 130 ft.

Railings and other ship machinery can also be seen on an overswim. Once again, take care to keep track of bottom time on this ship.

29 Family Beach

Family Beach, also known as Dogleg Reef and Hobie Beach, is a place where the whole family can enjoy the underwater world. To get there, drive down the breakwater about a mile until you come to a large stand of ironwood trees on the left. A short climb over the rocks will put you on a sandy beach. This area is a favorite spot for picnics and other family activities. Facing the harbor, the reef area richest in coral growth starts to the right. Its outline is obvious as it extends out and then to the left in a dogleg similar to that of a golf course. To get there, wade out to the drop-off in front of the beach. A sparsely covered ledge drops off to about 25 ft of sandy bottom.

This is a leisurely dive that allows divers plenty of bottom time. There are coral nooks and crannies that hide octopi and eels. Wrasses, damsels and parrotfish are common and there are various clownfish colonies scattered throughout. One large concentration of anemones and clownfish is particularly photogenic. It sits in

Location: Glass Breakwater
Depth Range: 2-60 ft (.6-18 meters)
Access: Beach or boat
Expertise Rating: Novice

about 4 ft next to an artistic stand of fire coral. The anemones are magenta and one-stripe clownfish dart in and out of them frantically, creating many photo opportunities.

There is sunken car here too. It is a Toyota, in case you're curious, although the story of its demise remains a mystery. Currents are rarely a problem here, although (like all harbor dives) silt can reduce visibility on windy days. There is a jet ski operation here that can be very disruptive, and its guests don't always follow instructions. It is best to snorkel here when it is not operating.

Family Beach offers healthy plate-like corals and hidden anemones.

30 American Tanker

This old water barge is a remnant of the war days and is the first wreck many people dive on Guam. It is accessible by shore about halfway down the breakwater after a precarious hike down a cliff and across some large boulders. By boat, two buoys normally mark the ship, so it is easy to find.

Location: Glass Breakwater
Depth Range: 35-95 ft (11 29 meters)
Access: Beach or Boat
Expertise Rating: Novice

Fish congregate on the tanker and there is a large pilothouse and some cables on the deck. Encrusting invertebrates grow along the side of the ship.

Do not penetrate this wreck. There have been some serious accidents from people trying to poke around inside. It silts up very easily. Also, the ship was a barge, so the interior is huge, dark and dangerous and there's really nothing of any visual or historical value inside. Some air pockets formed from dive bubbles are inside the wheelhouse. You can go up inside them to talk, but do not take your regulator out of your mouth to breath the air as it is toxic. Divers have passed out and have had to be rescued from breathing this bad air. This is an uncomplicated, fun dive on a big wreck. Explore the rudder and look for sea turtles along the deep side. This is also an interesting night dive with many small nudibranchs climbing about.

The world's largest nudibranch was found here on the sloping reef.

Wheelhouse and holds at the American Tanker.

31 Seabee Junkyard

Almost at the end of the breakwater is a lone tree where you can park to visit this site. It's dubbed the Seabee Junkyard for its role as dumping ground for bulldozers, amtracs, pipes and a lot other junk. In addition to all the vehicular debris, remnants of the *Caribia*—a large ocean liner that drifted into the harbor mouth as it was being towed to Taiwan for salvage—are scattered about.

Location: Apra Harbor
Depth Range: 40-130 ft (12-40 meters)
Access: Beach or Boat
Expertise Rating: Novice

This is a good dive for almost level of diver as it is shallow and there is rarely a current.

It can be reached by carefully climbing down the cliffside, or by boat if you anchor in the shallow water below the tree. The land slopes sharply down and then flattens out at about 25 ft. There are small coral heads and an amtrac that is partially buried. Presumably it was already sunken when the breakwater was built and was covered with some of the fill material.

Set compass headings and do some natural navigation. Four bulldozers are in close proximity to one another and one large amtrac is still in good shape with room for a diver to sit in the driver's seat. Truck beds and wheels are present. Lots of other things dumped as scrap here now provide habitat for fish and invertebrates.

Old war artifacts are found all over Seabee Junkyard.

32 Hidden Reef

Nestled near the mouth of the harbor is a reef with lots of sea anemones, pyramid butterflyfish and platy corals. This was a real showplace until the 1993 earthquake, when some of the elaborate coral formations got pretty well broken up. Few divers visit this little-known site, so it is still a nice reef with lots to see.

Location: Near Apra Harbor mouth
Depth Range: 40-100 ft (12-30 meters)
Access: Boat
Expertise Rating: Intermediate

At about 80 ft there's a vehicle that appears to be the sort of machine capable of ferrying airplanes around a tarmac. No doubt dumped during or shortly after the war, it has nice vase sponges on it and yellowtail basslets.

The upper reef has a large selection of sea anemones with skunk clowns and three-spot damsels. Many fish muster here to feed. On occasion, a shark will appear. Large jacks and dogtooth tuna have also been seen swimming past this reef.

The Big One

On August 8, 1993 Guam was rocked by the worst earthquake to hit the region in nearly a century. Measuring 8.2 on the Richter scale, the minute-long jolt resulted in 60 injuries, but fortunately no deaths.

Guam's frequent typhoons were partially responsible for protecting the island, as housing codes require all structures to be able to withstand 150-mile/hour winds. The housing codes saved many houses from quake destruction.

The quake originated deep in the Mariana Trench, where seismic activity is common, but because the activity is buffered by the world's greatest ocean depth, its effects are seldom felt on the islands. The quake of '93 was certainly a jarring exception.

TIM ROCK

Despite coral destruction during the 1993 earthquake, the reef is now recovering nicely.

33 Fingers Reef

This reef on the Orote Peninsula side near the mouth of the harbor juts out into the channel and is loaded with nice corals and lots of fish, which make excellent photo subjects for those who want to get a full portfolio of Pacific species. This is a daily second stop for many dive boats coming back from the Blue Hole, The Crevice or another harbor dive.

To avoid crowds, come here after 4 pm as the sun begins to set. This is also a very pleasant early morning dive as fish are plentiful and easy to observe. The water will also be calm and the reef will be well-lit.

Location: South harbor
Depth Range: 15-80 ft (5-24 meters)
Access: Boat
Expertise Rating: Novice

This reef has many fingers of coral that hold large sea anemone colonies, starfish, tunicates and other invertebrates. It is a good night dive, when many shrimps and crabs come out of hiding.

TIM ROCK

A wide variety of fish visit Fingers Reef.

34 Rock's Reef

This is a favorite spot for fish and anemone photography. Healthy corals and some unique deeper formations make this a fine location for all kinds of diving and snorkeling.

It basically encompasses the area between GabGab Beach and Fingers Reef and can hold great surprises. Schools of unicornfish, squid schools and big tuna come in along this sloping, coral-covered wall.

Many reefs have formed over the last 50 years after Navy ships were crowded into the harbor during the WWII. This site has some deep war artifacts, and a close look at the reef structure reveals the famous Coke-bottle base. Ships would

Location: West of GabGab
Depth Range: 15-80 ft (5-24 meters)
Access: Beach or Boat
Expertise Rating: Novice

dump their garbage while at anchor and many mounds of vintage Coca-Cola bottles (from 1943 and '44) accumulated as a result. After the big earthquake, this unstable base cracked to reveal the bottles on many reefs, including the deep reefs off Rock's Reef.

Clown triggerfish like to hang out at Rock's.

A diver checks out the unusual coral forms.

35 GabGab Beach

This is a great spot for a picnic, snorkel, dive and general water relaxation. This is the Navy's family recreation beach. There is a protected saltwater pool that is used for dive training as well as swimming. A lifeguard is usually on duty. Access to the area changes according to command and world affairs. If public access is not allowed, get someone to sponsor you on a beach dive or snorkel. If you dive by boat, no permission is needed.

This reef has great shallow coral valleys and some nice mini-walls. Sea turtles sometimes rest at the eastern end of the reef. There is also a small cave that occasionally holds an immense bull jack.

Location: Southern Apra shore
Depth Range: 10-80 ft (3-24 meters)
Access: Beach
Expertise Rating: Novice

This reef has many beautiful sea anemones and a good variety of fish species. At night, this dive reveals nocturnal invertebrates like some seldom–seen nudibranchs and a host of different shrimp and crabs.

TIM ROCK

GabGab is a favorite spot for large anemones and the tiny shrimp that live in their tentacles.

36 GabGab II Reef

This dive can be done by navigating from GabGab Beach or by boat. During most of the day, the *Atlantis* tourist submarine operates on this reef. A support boat and a commuter boat buzz about overhead as well as the sub that comes up and down. It can be a busy site; keep an eye out for the sub as it is quite silent.

Location: Off Apra south shore
Depth Range: 30-90 ft (9-27 meters)
Access: Beach or Boat
Expertise Rating: Intermediate

This reef is healthy on the whole but suffered some damage a few years back when a Navy contractor tried to move a huge mooring chain and scraped the reeftop. The University of Guam Marine Lab was called in to transplant corals and the experiment has been fairly successful, although it will take several decades to fully recover. This is a good place to observe the results of coral transplanting, a relatively new idea in the marine biology world.

The reef has lots of fish due to fish feeding by the submarine divers. A number of really big bull jacks show up when feeding commences but stay warily in the periphery when the feeding does not take place. There is also a large turtle that makes his home here part of the year.

Watch out for the *Atlantis*, a tourist sub that quietly cruises over the reef.

37 Western Shoals

Western Shoals provides an opportunity to experience Guam's coral world year round. Marked by a large cement block on its northern end, this reef is a honeycombed combination of branching and plate-like corals.

Many of the sponges at Western Shoals are quite large in comparison to those found on the outer reefs. They provide shelter for various Pacific reef fish.

Location: East harbor shoals
Depth Range: 10-80 ft (3-24 meters)
Access: Boat
Expertise Rating: Novice

A typical dive starts shallow. Staghorn coral covers much of the reeftop and

TIM ROCK

Western Shoals features deep coral canyons and a garden of vase sponges.

schools of blue chromis make the water shimmer in brilliant shades of blue.

On descent, notice the many cuts and crevices layered on the coral. Hidden in the recesses are Moorish idols, trumpetfish (some brilliant yellow) and curious soldierfish. The underside of the coral is festooned with encrusting sponges in yellow, purple and orange. Sea anemones with skunk clownfish and large carpet anemones with two-stripe clowns reside at 40 ft.

Even though visibility can be low here, it is a pleasant dive that reef lovers should enjoy.

38 Dry Dock Reef

This nice reef near the dry dock facility is one of the original harbor reefs but is not dived much. Ships moved past this reef to the inner harbor for many years and some didn't make it. One that fell to its sudden demise here was a vintage ship from the 1800s with a wooden hull and brass sides. Little is left of this ship but the observant history buff can find small pieces at the northeast end of the reef.

The west end of the reef is a mini-wall that is loaded with staghorn coral at the top and lots of unusual invertebrates. This is a fine night dive as there are lots of cracks and crevices worth exploring that hold clams, oysters and crabs.

Look for juvenile fish in the many staghorn beds. Some overgrown buoy chains on the south side and some nice valleys hold schools of fish and bright yellow trumpetfish.

Location: Near Harbor Dry Dock
Depth Range: 5-55 ft (1.5-17 meters)
Access: Boat
Expertise Rating: Novice

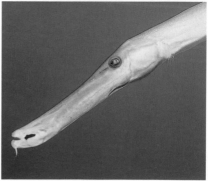

TIM ROCK

Look for trumpetfish on the overgrown buoy chains.

Diving in Rota

Just a 20-minute commuter plane hop from Guam opens up a hole new world of diving. Rota, the southernmost island of the Commonwealth of the Northern Marianas, is a ruggedly beautiful island with a low population density and exceptionally clear water. Divers need a valid passport to enter, as Rota is a different political entity. Virtually all other conditions found on Guam apply.

The Northern Marianas island chain extends far north and is comprised of "low" coral uplift and volcanic islands with coastlines ranging from

An aerial view of the Rota Resort golf course, the only one on the island.

TIM ROCK

A natural swimming hole on Rota's west coast.

rugged rocky cliffs to wide, white and black sand beaches. Inland areas are mostly forested with both indigenous and introduced species. Some islands are fringed with coral reefs that enclose clear shallow lagoons. Limestone caves and marine grottoes are found on all of the main islands, and many of the northern islands are still geologically active.

TIM ROCK

Be sure to visit Rota's wild bird sanctuary and rookery.

Rota has one of the finest seabird sanctuaries in the Pacific. Natural swimming holes, long, untouched sandy beaches, the rugged Sabana plateau, thrusting limestone cliffs and deep dripstone-filled caves are natural attractions. The Taisican Family Nature Trail, located high in the hills, is a favorite site for nature lovers who want to see local flora and take a brisk walk.

Despite Rota's proximity to Guam, the brown tree snake does not plague the island. Because of this, the islands are blessed with a profusion of tropical shrubs and over 40 species of birds.

Underwater, the surrounding coral reefs abound with fish of every description and color, as well as marine turtles and manta rays. The ocean waters are regularly visited by several species of large game fish such

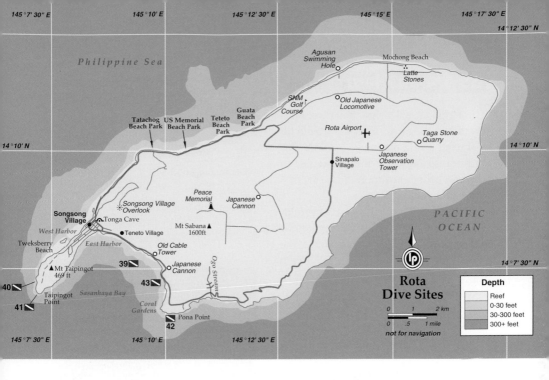

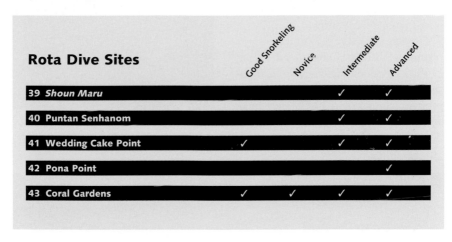

Rota Dive Sites	Good Snorkeling	Novice	Intermediate	Advanced
39 *Shoun Maru*			✓	✓
40 Puntan Senhanom			✓	✓
41 Wedding Cake Point	✓		✓	✓
42 Pona Point				✓
43 Coral Gardens	✓	✓	✓	✓

as marlin, mahi-mahi, tuna, barracuda and ulua. Rota has a selection of hard corals on the fringing reefs, sea fans and lace corals along the steep outer drop-offs. Schools of barracuda and jacks can be seen in the blue water. Fascinating caves with shafts of sunlight pouring through are found at relatively shallow depths, along with some WWII remnants, including those of a large freighter.

Rota has a nice variety of small hotels and local restaurants even though the main village, Songsong, retains a distinctively slow pace. This pristine little isle offers a great variety of diving in exceptionally clear water.

39 *Shoun Maru*

This freighter sunk in less than three minutes after an American aerial torpedo hit it during a raid on June 23, 1944. The ship was sitting at the end of a cable run used to bring phosphate down from a mine in the hills of Rota.

Location: East harbor, Sasanhaya Bay
Depth Range: 50-110 ft (15-34 meters)
Access: Boat
Expertise Rating: Intermediate

Today, the *Shoun Maru* sits upright. Its side was blown away during a poor excuse for a salvage operation in the '60s, which exposed the huge steam engine that powered the 4500-ton freighter. Crinoids, soft leather corals and hard corals all adorn the outside of the ship.

Inside the ship are remnants of a truck and a bicycle, although locals say the ship had just been unloaded of supplies and ammunition and that nothing was on board when it went down.

Fusiliers sweep the bow and midships region and sharks are often found resting in the sand alongside the ship. Garden eels live in the sand near the stern. The prop and rudder on this ship seem huge and can be a dwarfing experience for divers.

Bow of the *Shoun Maru*.

A truck found in the cargo of the sunken *Shoun Maru*.

40 Puntan Senhanom

Rota's signature attraction may well be this cave located on the west side of Wedding Cake Peninsula. It is an easy dive when the swells are down and can be a great thrill whether it is your first time or a repeat visit. The water visibility and position of the sun change the character of the cave throughout the day. It is best to visit the cave in early afternoon. At around 2 pm the sun sends direct lighting through an opening in the back of the cave.

Location: West side of Wedding Cake
Depth Range: 30-80 ft (9-24 meters)
Access: Boat
Expertise Rating: Intermediate

You can enter the cave through the sea window, swim toward the back while looking for sea life and then surface through the shimmering shafts of light, filtered electric blue by the sea. The lava rock is rough and getting out of the water can mean a scrape or two, but it is fun to at least surface and talk in the open pool.

To exit, swim back toward the mouth but follow the wall on the right. There is another small tunnel with shelves along the wall. Sleeping whitetips have been found in here resting on a shelf. Encrusting sponges and marine life can be colorful, so use a light to bring out the brilliance. Many cowries live in the waters around Rota and this cave is a good spot to see them.

TIM ROCK

Shimmering light filters into the cave at Puntan Senhanom.

41 Wedding Cake Point

On the right day, this can be an awesome dive. The visibility is normally 200 ft or better. Huge boulders sit along the slope near the point and an impressive fan-covered wall and drop-off make the diver feel extremely small.

Location: Taipingot Point
Depth Range: 10-130 ft (3-40 meters)
Access: Boat
Expertise Rating: Intermediate

Approach the point quietly in order to see a large school of silvery skipjacks that seems to reside here. Rainbow runners may course by in schools as well; their curiosity will bring them close and reveal their silvery bodies. Sharks, mostly grey reef and whitetip, may also appear in the evenings and early mornings.

The water clarity here is amazingly deceptive and divers may find themselves much deeper than intended. Keep an eye on your gauges and an eye out to sea. I have seen sailfish and other pelagics at this point. There are some nice sea anemones on top of the boulders in the shallower waters. Currents can be a problem here, so be sure to carry a safety sausage in case you must surface away from the boat.

A steep outer wall and lots of anemones make Wedding Cake an interesting dive.

42 Pona Point

This site is found at the eastern end of Sasanhaya Bay and there are actually three good spots in the vicinity. One is the Pearlman Tunnel around the point along the eastern coast. Home to sleeping whitetip sharks, golden gorgonians and spotted cowries, the cave starts deep and rises to 20 ft with an opening to the sun. Waves crash along the sheer cliffline above and reverberate through the tunnel.

Location: Sasanhaya Bay
Depth Range: 10-90 ft (3-27 meters)
Access: Boat
Expertise Rating: Advanced

TIM ROCK

Sea fans decorate a coral bommie at Pona Point.

Outside, at about 90 ft, a ridge full of sea fans and fish life is another one of Rota's deceptively clear and inviting sites. Look for large red snappers and batfish. Whitetip sharks may be lurking here as well.

The Pona Point is devoid of heavy coral growth, but is an excellent spot to hang out and watch for deep-water fish and pelagics. Look for the current line and you will probably find a large school of barracuda. Schools of bat fish have also been sighted regularly here.

43 Coral Gardens

This site was once the showplace of the Northern Mariana Islands and it is still a nice spot to snorkel. A misguided attempt to dispose of old WWII ordnance by the U.S. Navy instead blasted portions of the reef and some remnants of WWII sub chasers, killed a few sea turtles and created a crater in the sea floor.

After surveying the damage and a great deal of uproar, an independent contractor (aptly named Bombs Away) was hired to quietly remove the rest of the old ordnance without explosions or incidents.

This was a few years ago and the area is coming back slowly but it is a good reminder that once a great resource is lost,

Location: East harbor shoals
Depth Range: 10-70 ft (3-21 meters)
Access: Boat
Expertise Rating: Novice

it may never be recovered. The upper reef is home to many colorful angel and butterflyfishes. It is good for snorkeling, a shallow second dive and for a night dive. Look for remnants of the sub chasers, both sunk in June of 1944.

Double saddle angelfish swim through the Coral Gardens.

TIM ROCK

Overview
of Yap

TIM ROCK

"When fishing, if you see a turtle's tail in front of your boat, you will have bad luck. But if the turtle's head is pointing toward you, your luck will be good."
– Yapese proverb

Yap is the most traditional Micronesian island, just a little over an hour's flight from Guam but worlds away in terms of culture. In the last few years, Yap has made cautious but progressive steps to cash in on Micronesia's growing popularity as a holiday destination. The results are new businesses popping up to cater to the visitor industry, making Yap a "convenient adventure" of sorts.

Tradition plays an important role in life on the islands of Yap. The people here are very proud of their unique culture and have resisted major changes or modernization. The pavement ends as you leave the town and head to the villages. Here life continues much as it has for hundreds of years.

History

Yap's human history dates back to about AD 200 but may go further as there have been few archaeological studies about the islands or their unique inhabitants. Yapese are known as great ocean navigators. Residents of the outer atolls still sail vast distances in open canoes hewn from the immense trunks of breadfruit trees. Each ocean-going canoe is built by hand using adzes and other manual carving tools. On some islands, outboards have taken the place of these great canoes, but others still keep the tradition going strong.

Yapese magic was considered to be very powerful and the Yapese once controlled a far-reaching empire ranging from the Marianas to the vast outer atolls.

Today, Yap state consists of the main high islands of Yap Proper (Wa'ab) and the outer islands (Remetau). A strong caste system was once in effect, with the higher castes living in the villages of the high islands. These castes are still followed loosely today, but have broken down over the years and the

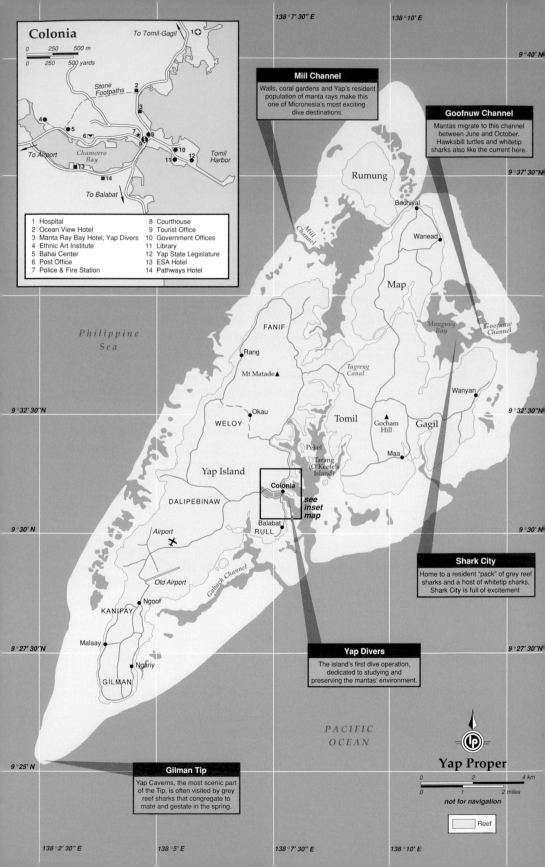

Colonia

0   250   500 m
0   250   500 yards

To Tomil-Gagil

Stone Footpaths

Chamorro Bay

To Airport

To Balabat

Tomil Harbor

1 Hospital
2 Ocean View Hotel
3 Manta Ray Bay Hotel, Yap Divers
4 Ethnic Art Institute
5 Bahai Center
6 Post Office
7 Police & Fire Station
8 Courthouse
9 Tourist Office
10 Government Offices
11 Library
12 Yap State Legislature
13 ESA Hotel
14 Pathways Hotel

Mill Channel
Walls, coral gardens and Yap's resident population of manta rays make this one of Micronesia's most exciting dive destinations.

Goofnuw Channel
Mantas migrate to this channel between June and October. Hawksbill turtles and whitetip sharks also like the current here.

Shark City
Home to a resident "pack" of grey reef sharks and a host of whitetip sharks, Shark City is full of excitement

Yap Divers
The island's first dive operation, dedicated to studying and preserving the mantas' environment.

Gilman Tip
Yap Caverns, the most scenic part of the Tip, is often visited by grey reef sharks that congregate to mate and gestate in the spring.

Philippine Sea

PACIFIC OCEAN

Rumung

Bechiyal

Wanead

Map

FANIF

Rang

Mt Matade▲

Mungnuy Bay

Goofnuw Channel

Tagreng Canal

Wanyan

Okau

WELOY

Tomil

Gocham Hill ▲

Gagil

Maa

Yap Island

Pekel

Tarang (O'Keefe's Island)

Colonia

see inset map

DALIPEBINAW

Balabat

RULL

Airport

Old Airport

Gabach Channel

Ngoof

KANIFAY

Malaay

Ngariy

GILMAN

Yap Proper

0   2   4 km
0   1   2 miles

not for navigation

☐ Reef

138°7'30" E
138°10' E
9°40' N
9°37'30"N
9°32'30"N
9°30' N
9°27'30"N
9°25' N
138°2'30" E
138°5' E
138°7'30" E
138°10' E

chiefs do not posses absolute power as they once did.

Yapese dress is still traditional, not so much in town but in the small villages. Men still wear loincloths and women wear grass skirts or lava-lavas. Toplessness is not considered offensive on Yap, but a woman in a miniskirt is as shocking as a topless woman in a U.S. shopping center. Things are a little more lax in the capital, Colonia.

When exploring Yap it is wise to hire a guide. Permission must be asked of each village chief before entering certain areas and a local guide can smooth things over considerably.

Geography

Yap is part of the Federated States of Micronesia (FSM). The entire state consists of scattered atolls. The capital island, Yap Proper, is actually five islands of old volcanic origin surrounded by a huge barrier reef and connected by mangrove-lined waterways and human-made bridges. As the outer islands are minimally developed and hard to reach, most diving is done in Yap Proper.

Yap's southern tip features steep ocean walls and deep reef canyons. The north has broad coral reef flats that gradually slope into the sea. Yap has many deep, colorful channels that provide for unique and interesting diving. Both Miil Channel and Goofnuw Channel feature great populations of manta rays, the presence of which have made Yap diving so special.

Betel Nut

"If betel nut juice from your mouth accidentally drips on you, it is a sign of good luck."
— Yapese belief

Everyone, but everyone, in Yap chews *"buw"* or betel nut. Small stores do a good business selling zip-lock bags of betel nuts and pepper leaves for $2.50 "a plastic."

Betel nut is split open while green, sprinkled with dry coral lime, wrapped in pepper leaves and then chewed. It produces a mild high that lasts about 10 minutes. Sometimes tobacco, or tobacco soaked in vodka, is added.

Betel nut turns the saliva bright red and stains the teeth red and eventually black. It's the lime that stimulates the flow of saliva. Once called "a dentist's nightmare" by Westerners, recent findings indicate that chewing betel nut may actually help prevent cavities.

Not that this would sway the Yapese one way or the other. They start chewing *buw* at a very early age and continue as long as they are able to chew—perhaps even longer.

According to old timers, even ghosts chew betel nut. If a sailing canoe was to stop for no obvious reason in the middle of a lagoon, the sailor would prepare a special betel nut mixture, wrap it in extra leaves and tie it up tightly with many knots. He would then throw it overboard and sail away easily, while the ghost who'd been holding the canoe was busy untying the knots.

Yap Practicalities

Climate

Yap's climate, like most of Micronesia, is uniformly warm and humid. The evening temperatures average 72°F (22°C) in the evenings and 86°F (31°C) during the day. Rainfall averages 120 inches (304 cm) a year, but is seasonal. The transitional months of May, June and November are considered peak typhoon season. An annual average of three typhoons hit Yap, and severe storms can wreak massive devastation in the outer islands. The most damaging parts of storms tend to miss Yap Proper, a fact which many people still attribute to the island's strong "magic."

For good diving, the western side of the island—especially the Gilman area—is normally protected most of the year. Visibility is affected by runoff, so rainy season months mean lower visibility. Tides can vary greatly at full moon. Visibility is best at high morning, incoming tide. Currents affect the channel dive sites, and can be strong along the deep outer reef sites, making drift diving a real pleasure.

STEPHANIE BRENDL

Shoreline near the Village View Hotel.

Language

There are four indigenous languages in Yap: Yapese, Ulithian, Woleaian and Satawalese. English is the official language of the FSM and is commonly spoken and understood, but Yapese is the main language of the people. Many elderly Yapese are also fluent in Japanese.

Getting There

Getting to Yap requires some planning ahead. Guam is served daily by major carriers from all over the Asian region and from the U.S. through Honolulu. Travelers must then connect to Yap via Guam or Manila through Continental Micronesia, which has only a few flights weekly to Yap. The flight from Guam takes about 90 minutes.

Getting Around

Taxis are cheap and plentiful for getting around town. Colonia is small, so walking is also advisable and pleasant. To travel to the outer villages, it is best to rent a car. Reserve a car through your hotel before you arrive to ensure you will get one. Do not play the radio or cassette player loudly while traveling through villages as it is considered rude. The bus system brings people into town to work in the mornings and takes them to the villages at night but is not of major use to tourists.

Entry

A valid passport and ongoing airline ticket are necessary for entry to Yap. Visas are not required for visits of up to 30 days. Entry permits can be extended for up to 90 days, or 365 days for U.S. citizens. Entry authorization for longer than 30 days must be obtained in advance from Immigration and Labor, FSM National Government, Colonia, Pohnpei, FSM 96941.

Money

The official currency in Yap is the U.S. dollar; have some on hand for restaurants and shopping. Credit cards are accepted at most hotels and at a limited number of stores and restaurants. The two commercial banks in Yap—the Bank of the FSM and the Bank of Hawaii—are open on weekdays. Otherwise hotel staff can usually cash travelers checks for you.

The Land of Stone Money

Legend has it that the ancient navigator Anagumang set sail in search of the ideal stone to be used as Yapese currency. On Palau's Rock Islands he found a hard crystalline limestone that the Yapese quarried into huge flat discs. Holes were carved in the center so logs could be slipped through and the stones were then lugged down to barges and towed by canoe the 250 miles back to Yap.

With their weighty cargo, entire expeditions were sometimes lost in storms at sea. The most valuable stones were not necessarily the largest, but those that were transported at the highest cost of human lives. These stones commonly bore the names of the lost mariners.

Stone money, which the Yapese call rai, can range up to 12 ft in diameter and weigh as much as five tons. The Japanese civilian government counted 13,281 coins in 1929.

Although single pieces of stone money are commonly seen throughout Yap, most stone money is kept in "banks" lined up along village pathways. The money is not moved, even when ownership changes. Stone money remains in use today for some traditional exchanges, although the U.S. dollar settles most commonplace transactions.

A Yapese man stands beside large pieces of ancient stone money.

TIM ROCK

What to Bring

General Supplies Local stores stock basic food, but little in the way of specialty items. Some fruits, canned meats, cereals and canned fruits and vegetables are available. Snack foods are also in supply. Milk is canned. Batteries and other imported units can be old. If you need anything not in the basic category, from booze to vitamins, bring it with you. Lightweight clothing and T-shirts are sold around town.

Dive Related Equipment Repairs and parts are extremely limited except for basic items like mask straps, o-rings, etc. Try to bring all necessary equipment except weights. If a personal piece of dive gear should fail, it is possible to find a replacement through rental or purchase. Only a dive skin is necessary for warmth and protection from abrasions or stings.

What to Wear

It never gets cold in Yap, so bring only lightweight, casual clothing. Formal wear is considered unnecessary and impractical. (A former Governor once proposed establishing a law forbidding the wearing of ties in Yap!)

Men will find slacks and a Hawaiian-style shirt appropriate for even the most formal occasion. A cap, shorts, light pants, sport shirts and T-shirts make a good basic wardrobe. Flip-flops are acceptable anywhere on Yap.

For women, lightweight cotton dresses, longer shorts, slacks, blouses and skirts make the best island wear. Toplessness is common and socially acceptable, but showing the thigh is not. Short shorts and bikinis are a no-no and after swimming you should cover up.

Time

Like Guam, Yap is 10 hours ahead of GMT/UTC.

Underwater Photography

Yap Divers has a facility called **Manta Visions** that has film for sale, E-6 processing, some video editing and some repair available. It is the only such dependable photographic operation in Yap. Camera rental and underwater photography instruction, like manta photography courses, combine biology and other fascinating aspects of manta life. Bring all necessary supplies like film, batteries and back-up bodies just in case the film supply ship hasn't arrived for a few weeks.

Business Hours

Most dive operations are open year round. General stores are open from about 9 am to 6 pm during the week but most close on weekends when the locals leave town to visit to their villages. Colonia is very quiet over the weekend except for some local bars, which can be a lot fun. There are numerous FSM holidays and U.S. holidays are also observed, so government offices and stores may be closed when you don't expect it. Yap Day is always the first day of March and is well worth attending.

Accommodations

Colonia is still a small, relatively quiet community. It is the center of government for the island. Well-established hotels offer reasonable rates, clean rooms and good restaurants. The **ESA** and the **Ocean View** cater to the business traveler, while the **Pathways** and the **Manta Ray Bay Hotel** are a little more upscale. **Village View** is located well out of town and is a beachside retreat for those who want to really get away. The Manta Ray caters to divers and dive groups. It has spacious rooms and is located adjacent to the dive shop and dock of Yap Divers.

For a truly unique glimpse into the rich culture of Yap, "home-stays" with families in local villages can be arranged in advance by the Yap Visitors' Bureau (YVB). If you are planning to stay with a local family during your visit to Yap, you may want to bring along a few photographs from your homeland and some small gifts for the family members.

Visits to Yap's pristine outer islands can also be arranged in advance by the YVB.

Dining & Food

Yap has a number of unpretentious, basic restaurants. Fresh fish dishes tend to be popular with visitors. The **Manta Ray Bay Bar & Grill** offers Yap's only fine dining experience as chef Bill Munn creates a new menu every evening. The fresh blackened ahi is rapidly becoming one of Munn's most famous creations. All eateries are located in the downtown Colonia area. Restaurants and bars are open until 10:30 pm.

Staple foods of the island include taro, yam, breadfruit, sweet potatoes and coconut. The main source of protein comes from fish, crab, clams and pork. Local foods and fresh vegetables can be found at the **Waab Mak'uuf Market** and at some local stores.

Drinking Permits Visitors staying longer than 30 days are required to obtain a *Yap State Alcoholic Beverage Drinking Permit,* issued by the Chief of Police for $5. Good for one year, the permit can be a unique memento of your visit to Yap.

Shopping

Shopping on Yap is limited but a keen eye may find some special handicrafts. There are four or five good local shops that have grass skirts, leis, carved storyboards and many other unique Yapese craft items. Also check in some of the small stores for lava-lavas and other island gems.

Yap Activities & Attractions

TIM ROCK

If there is a celebration scheduled in Yap, it is well worth watching. History, legends and stories are passed down by word of mouth and through song. Old and new songs and dances are performed at celebrations and are quite colorful and melodic.

Yap Day

Some folks come from the quiet shoreline villages set deep in the mangroves and some travel from the small outposts windblown by warm tropical winds. Others travel from neighboring islands to Yap, this tiny Micronesian outpost of tradition.

The island's cozy hotels fill up quickly. Visitors hail from Europe, Tokyo and other parts of Japan, the U.S. and a number of Micronesian and Marianas islands.

The occasion is Yap Day, an official state holiday held by the main island Yapese every March 1st. The attendees come to perform, listen to speeches and award ceremonies, and to view and photograph one of the last vestiges of true traditional culture. Yap residents and visitors alike take up ringside seats on the ground and gleefully snap photos of friends and relatives.

Aside from the dancing, a number of award ceremonies are held to recognize local anglers and farmers.

Island handicrafts are also judged and displayed. Finely woven baskets and skirts are made out of coconut fronds and pandanus leaves; it is a traditional art still practiced for anything from baskets and skirts to walls and roofs.

If you're in Micronesia, Yap Day is a celebration you won't want to miss.

Dance on Yap

Dances on Yap don't just happen and aren't oft repeated. The steps and the chants are intertwined and are practiced weeks and even months beforehand. Young girls learn the dance movements for the first time while teenagers are taught chants, being groomed to lead the group in later years.

There are four distinct types of Yapese dances: the bamboo dance, the marching dance, the sitting dance and the standing dance. Two of the dances are now performed by young men and women together, a modern diversion from traditional custom.

The marching dances and bamboo stick dances are for the young and very active. The sitting and the standing dances are more sedate in nature and are without exception performed by men and women separately.

The bamboo dance is incredibly entertaining to watch. Performed to a chant, the dancers' hips swing wildly and sensually while they move in and out of tight formations, constantly reforming. Throughout the dance, the dancers make contact with each others' sticks. These aren't the light taps tourists see in the local Polynesian hotel shows. High and low blows are dealt with vigor and considerable force. Many a thick bamboo pole splits in the woman's hands and has to be quickly replaced by a knowledgeable onlooker. This dance has its highs and lows with periods of fierce screams, concentrated movements and contact. An occasional knuckle suffers from an errant strike. But there are also smiles and giggles as the dancers release adrenaline built up from the incredible pace and frenzy of their work.

Dances may not be performed again for a long time—ranging from months to years to never again. There is a sort of retirement ritual a dance goes through; this is what makes the dances so special.

Dance on Yap is a colorful, energetic celebration of culture and tradition.

TIM ROCK

TIM RCCK

Sunset over Yap's freshwater lake.

The Outer Islands

Yap's outer islands are accessible only by freight boat or small commuter plane. Here people live a subsistence lifestyle. Women raise crops and men fish for the family. Some of the islanders still use large, traditional canoes, although most islanders now use power boats.

The vast majority of the reefs and lagoons of Yap's 134 islands remain completely unexplored. From the WWII wrecks preserved underwater at Ulithi to the miles of untouched reefs at Nguluan—an island between Yap and Palau—thousands of miles of still await exploration. A few local entrepreneurs are trying to start cave diving and other reef exploration on Fais. Diving in the outer islands is reported to be very good by yachting adventurers, but there is currently no organized dive operation of any kind on the outer Yap islands.

Bechiyal Cultural Center

A unique attraction in Yap, the Bechiyal Cultural Center displays some of the ancient money and other instruments used before the onset of the westerner in Yap. It is located north of Bechiyal on Map (pronounced Mop) island.

To get there, follow the road north to Map. Once there, you can park at the bottom of the hill on the right side. A river empties into the ocean, providing a scenic view of a palm-shrouded delta. Cross the log bridge that spans the small river and you will have entered Bechiyal village. The first house on the left is the chief's house. It is Yapese courtesy to ask permission before traipsing through someone's village, even if the walkway is wide and unobtrusive. There is also a store there. Tell the owner of your intentions and then buy a couple of cold drinks. The trail is jungled and you will find you will need the refreshment at the end of the hike. While walking, you can talk, but shouting and loud talking is considered rude behavior.

The walk in takes you past village stone money banks, copra-drying stands, village houses, coconut tree plantations and mangrove swamps. Overhead, noddies call in the trees. The walk can be done in about 20 minutes. Take a sweat band and mosquito repellent for total comfort.

This center is not glitzy—just a set of buildings on a quiet beach next to a family's house. It is still used to teach young Yapese men the traditional ways of building. Nearby is a modern guest house and arrangements can be made to stay overnight.

Local men gather to rebuild the roof of a meeting house.

Diving in Yap

TIM ROCK

Yap offers divers a glimpse of healthy reefs and unspoiled ocean. In these days of heavy tourism and worldwide reef destruction, viewing Yap's underwater world is a special experience that few divers will ever forget.

Yap is one of the most intriguing islands in Micronesia. Walls, coral gardens and a resident population of easily observed manta rays give Yap its claim to fame. But you can't just rent some tanks and go diving in Yap. All dives are boat dives, done with a local guide. Because the Yap reefs traditionally belong to a village or individual, permission must be granted to dive a certain area.

The real adventure in diving Yap is the sense of exploration. Some favorite and standard dive sites are rich in sea life and coral, but miles and miles of reefline and channels are yet to be explored.

Yap's big boast to the diving world is its guaranteed manta sighting program. For many years, fishermen hunting for a fish dinner near the Miil Channel reported frequent sightings of manta rays swimming by their boats. Fortunately, mantas are not considered a delicacy in Yap, so they were not hunted.

When diving opened up through Yap Divers in 1987, divemasters investigated this talk and sure enough, manta rays were everywhere. Years of observation have helped them understand the mantas' habits enough to allow the average sport diver to observe the animals without disturbing their natural routine.

The mantas in this channel, the species *Manta birostris*, are common throughout Micronesian channels and outer reefs. They have been observed in Pohnpei, Truk, Guam, Palau and other regional destinations, but not in such concentrations as in Yap.

The animals commonly range in size from 6 to 12 ft. They are harmless filter feeders, eating mainly plankton. They have tails but no barb as stingrays do. They can be seen individually or in schools.

In the long and winding Miil Channel, mantas visit the many cleaning stations where small fish—mostly cleaner wrasse—come out of the corals and rocks to scour the mantas of parasites. While the mantas hover at the top of the coral heads, divers can observe wrasse darting in and out of the rays' gills and syphonlike mouths.

The rays undergo a short cleaning session, gracefully swim away, but soon return for another cleaning. This can go on for hours, so patient divers have a good chance of seeing many different rays.

Yap is surrounded by a large barrier reef; inside the reef flat lagoon mangrove trees provide habitat for many juvenile sea creatures. The mangroves trap nutrients washing into the sea from the land via rivers and streams. These nutrients are then released with the flows of the tides.

The popular sites are located at Yap's southern tip and along the southern and southcentral coastline. Operators are always finding new dive sites in Yap, so ask what's new when you get there.

TIM ROCK

With pristine reefs and large concentrations of manta rays, Yap boasts excellent diving.

A diver checks out a giant growth of yellow cabbage corals.

TIM ROCK

Yap Walls & Reefs

	Good Snorkeling	Novice	Intermediate	Advanced
44 Eagle's Nest			✓	✓
45 Gilman Tip			✓	✓
46 Lionfish Wall	✓		✓	✓
47 Yap Caverns	✓	✓	✓	✓
48 Gilman Wall	✓		✓	✓
49 Magic Kingdom	✓	✓	✓	✓
50 Cabbage Patch			✓	✓
51 Spanish Walls	✓		✓	✓
52 Cherry Blossom Wall	✓	✓	✓	✓
53 Sunrise Reef	✓	✓	✓	✓
54 Goofnuw Mini Wall	✓		✓	✓

Yap Channels

	Good Snorkeling	Novice	Intermediate	Advanced
55 Goofnuw Channel	✓	✓	✓	✓
56 Shark City	✓	✓	✓	✓
57 Garden Eel Flats			✓	✓
58 Manta Cleaning Station	✓	✓	✓	✓
59 Manta Ridge	✓		✓	✓
60 Miil Point	✓		✓	✓
61 Spaghetti Factory				✓
62 Manta Ray Bay	✓		✓	✓

138°2'30" E   138°5' E   138°7'30" E   138°10' E

9°40' N   9°40' N

Philippine
Sea

9°37'30"N   9°37'30"N

Rumung

62

Bechiyal

61
60   Mill
59   Channel
58   Wanead   53
57

9°35' N   9°35' N

Map

FANIF   Munguuy   56 55 Goofnuw
                                             Bay   Channel 54

Rang

Mt Matade▲   *Tagreng*
                    Canal   Waniyan

9°32'30"N   Okau   Tomil   Gocham   9°32'30"N
              WELOY   Hill ▲   Gagil

              Pekel
              Tarang
              (O'Keefe's   Maa
              Island)

Yap Island

52   DALIPEBINAW   Colonia

              Balabat
9°30' N   RULL   9°30' N

51   Airport ✈

              Old Airport   *Gabach Channel*

50   KANIFAY   Ngoof

9°27'30"N Malaay ●   9°27'30"N

              Ngariy
49   GILMAN

48
                                    PACIFIC
47   *OCEAN*

46
45   LP
9°25' N   **Yap Proper**
                                           Dive Sites

44
                          0   2   4 km
                          0   1   2 miles
                              not for navigation

                              ▢ Reef

138°2'30" E   138°5' E   138°7'30" E   138°10' E

44 Eagle's Nest

Eagle's Nest is an easy drift dive along the barrier reef where schooling eagle rays are frequently sighted. The animals like to feed in a formation that almost resembles a military air squadron.

Location: Just south of Gilman Tip
Depth Range: 20-130 ft (6-40 meters)
Access: Boat
Expertise Rating: Intermediate

Eagle rays glide through Eagle's Nest.

At 50 ft, the level plateau has a large coral head, which is swept by currents that seem to attract eagle rays. They circle the coral and then swim out along the sandy plateau, following a spillway down to 130 ft.

Look for macro creatures in shallower water. Large coral outcrops provide good shelter for invertebrates and many juvenile fish.

As this side is exposed to the trade winds, the best diving here is May to November.

45 Gilman Tip

The Gilman Tip shows little sign of being adversely affected by humans. The intense and undamaged coral growth attracts a large number of fish that display an innocent curiosity when divers approach. This Tip juts out more than two miles from the Yap mainland, representing the southernmost point on the Yap barrier reef.

Location: South barrier reef, Gilman Tip
Depth Range: 20-130 ft (6-40 meters)
Access: Boat
Expertise Rating: Intermediate

This site has always been popular with fishers and divers alike. It is a drop-off where two currents converge. The fish and pelagic action here is usually good to sometimes spectacular. On a single dive, you could see schools of huge bumphead

Hard corals line the reef top at Gilman Tip.

TIM ROCK

A giant cluster of bulb sea anemones on Gilman Tip.

parrotfish, sleeping whitetip sharks, grey reef sharks, moray eels, rotund groupers, a school of copper sweepers, large triggerfish and a kaleidoscope of reef fish in incredible hues and colors.

More often than not, the dives here are drift dives. Gilman Tip offers a breath-taking sheer vertical face covered with a rich array of hard, soft coral and gorgonian corals. This is a place to see golden and multicolored crinoids on top of sea fans and coral heads. Pilot whales sometime swim through here. For pristine coral and good fish watching, the Tip has a lot.

46 Lionfish Wall

This dive can be done anywhere from 20 to 130 ft with the bottom coming up at around 120 ft in some places. Sharks are frequently seen resting along the bottom. Big groupers can be spotted along with snappers, and lots of bigeyes and soldierfish in the crevices. Lionfish, with white, flowing appendages, hide in the holes and under the ledges of the wall. They feed on small crabs and shrimps and they can inflict a painful sting, so be careful. They will stand their ground, so don't harass them. Another scorpionfish, the leaf scorpionfish, is found at about 20 ft near the

Location: South barrier reef, Gilman Tip
Depth Range: 20-130 ft (6-40 meters)
Access: Boat
Expertise Rating: Intermediate

top of Lionfish Wall where Yap Caverns begin. This brown little critter looks like a leaf blowing in the current, except that it doesn't float away. The leaf scorpionfish is relatively uncommon in Micronesia and may also be colored red, black or a silvery white.

Large anemones, including a big cluster of bulb anemones, cling to the wall sides. The reeftop is good for decompressing.

Look for big boxfish that swimming in groups of three or more. The current can change quickly here, sometimes making it necessary to reverse directions, but it is normally an easy drift dive.

Lionfish find refuge in the crevices of of Lionfish Wall.

47 Yap Caverns

Yap Caverns, the most scenic part of the Gilman Tip, is where the whitetip sharks snooze. The Lionfish Wall gives way to an undersea desert punctuated by imposing coral heads. The white, sandy floor of this site is in about 65 ft, sloping upward to about 20 ft. A quiet and slow approach will allow divers to observe whitetip sharks lazing about near overhangs and along the sandy slopes. There appear to be cleaning stations at some spots in this sandy maze and the sharks and other fish such as trevally jacks benefit from the action of the smaller cleaner wrasses.

Location: South barrier reef, Gilman Tip
Depth Range: 20-70 ft (6-21 meters)
Access: Boat
Expertise Rating: Novice

As many as 20 grey reef sharks hang out at 80 ft near the northwest side of the caverns. They mate and bear young in May and June. The males can be aggressive, putting on quite a display (probably a protective reaction) when the females are around, giving divers an action-packed, slightly scary show. Stay above 90 ft to allow them their territory. At times, baby sharks swim within the protection of the larger sharks. Witnessing this kind of behavior of marine animals in the wild is a special experience.

The caverns themselves are great fun to swim through as most have well-lit tunnels that are easy to pass through. The tunnels are usually shark-free because the whitetips don't hang around when divers show up. Starfish and copper sweepers hide inside the holes.

Yap Caverns offers great opportunities for colorful macrophotography.

Yap's deeper dives are home to groups of whitetip and grey reef sharks that rest on the sandy bottom.

48 Gilman Wall

This dive is found at the north end of the Yap Caverns and features lots of big crevices. Turtles are often found swimming or resting here and moray eels might peer out and surprise you. While you swim through the crevice looking for invertebrates to photograph, don't be surprised if a 7-ft moray comes swimming to greet you. Once it satisfies its curiosity, it will likely pop right back into one of the many holes that dot the crevice wall. Also look for the beautiful clown triggerfish

Location: Southwest of Gilman Tip
Depth Range: 20-100 ft (6-30 meters)
Access: Boat
Expertise Rating: Intermediate

along the sloped wall. This also is a good spot for sea anemones.

TIM ROCK

A hawksbill turtle gracefully swims by the Gilman Wall.

49 Magic Kingdom

The Magic Kingdom can be a truly magical experience. The fish and coral life here is healthy and active. At any moment you could be greeted by grey reef sharks, roving dogtooth tuna, schools of barracuda or hawksbill turtles.

The reef slopes gently to a shelf at about 50 ft and then slopes again to about 110 ft. The coral becomes sparse at about 120 ft; diving in the 30 to 60 ft range should be the norm.

Location: West side of Gilman Tip

Depth Range: 20-90 ft (6-27 meters)

Access: Boat

Expertise Rating: Novice

On the upper reaches of the Tip, branching corals are abundant. Pyramid butterflyfish frequent these patches and light up the reef as their white and gold colors flicker in the gentle surge. Hovering above, close to the surface, are thick schools of sharpnose barracuda. Just the sheer numbers of these timid fish can be awesome. Schools of the larger, black-striped great barracuda also come in to peer at divers before returning to the deep water.

Some large coral heads covered with bright encrusting sponges and platy corals dot the reef landscape. Flowing formations of lettuce corals house blue damsels. Brain and other acropora corals grow into and over one another in competition for prime feeding space.

An occasional whitetip shark will coast by or can be seen resting on a coral ledge. On the coral heads, one can see plenty of macrophotography subjects including cleaner shrimp, tunicate colonies and yellow and black crinoids propped on top of the lettuce corals.

This is one of the richest areas for coral growth in the diving world. The competition for space is intense on this reef and it is one of the most marvelous places to observe hard coral growth in the marine kingdom. Treat it gently and take lots of pictures.

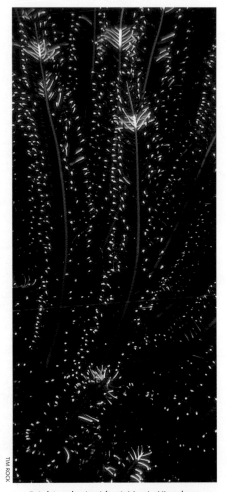

TIM ROCK

Bright red crinoids at Magic Kingdom.

50 Cabbage Patch

The actual Cabbage Patch site does not have cabbage corals, as you might expect, but is a vertical wall that drops to about 80 ft and then slopes deeply into the blue.

Location: West side of Gilman Tip
Depth Range: 20-100 ft (6-30 meters)
Access: Boat
Expertise Rating: Intermediate

Visibility can be tricky here as outgoing tides can bring nutrients from the lagoon into the water and reduce it considerably. But on a good day, it's over 100 ft.

This place has a lot of cuts and crevices with hard corals, or leather corals with their flowing polyps outstretched to feed.

This is a good spot to look for feeding and resting sea turtles. A barracuda school may also come in to greet you.

A barracuda school comes in from deeper waters for a visit to the Cabbage Patch.

51 Spanish Walls

Divers begin this dive by descending on acres and acres of staghorn coral. Thick schools of chromis (damselfishes) that hover above in the coral branches, catching food from the ebbs and flows of the current. Many different sea anemones are also nestled in with a variety of clownfish darting in and out of the maze.

Location: South, central coast
Depth Range: 20-100 ft (6-30 meters)
Access: Boat
Expertise Rating: Intermediate

The Spanish Walls are covered with soft corals.

A little deeper masses of plate corals cascade down, punctuated by huge overhangs. Under these ledges lie groupers, bigeyes and squirrelfish. Sea fans grow in the cratered holes and tunnels of the formations. Delicate lace corals also accent the sponge-encrusted site.

If you swim along the coral-rich slope, you'll arrive at the Spanish Walls, so named for an abundance of lace corals that resemble Spanish lace.

Flashy blue fusiliers and brilliant yellowtail fusiliers run up and down the reef, creating great photo opportunities. It is not unusual for schools of barracuda to come in for a look. Reef whitetip sharks sleep on the hard corals. Large cascading falls of plate-like corals appear at 70 ft. Soft corals and lace corals grow in the pocked overhangs following the rich slope.

Leather coral feeding at night.

The corals are pastel colors and can be seen up inside the wall. Watch your bubbles, however, as they can be abrasive to the soft coral. There is lots of shallow fish life, so decompression is entertaining.

52 Cherry Blossom Wall

Named for the many colorful tunicate colonies blossoming on fairly sheer wall, each crook and crevice on this dive holds surprises. Filter-feeding polychaete worms of various sizes and shapes are littered all over coral heads. The tiny

Location: South, central coast

Depth Range: 30-110 ft (9-34 meters)

Access: Boat

Expertise Rating: Novice

The "buffalo of the sea," the bumphead parrotfish is easy to recognize.

invertebrates come in colors of shocking blue and outrageous yellow. This is an excellent macrophotography spot. The top of the wall is nice for fish watching and there are some large anemones here. In the distance, bumphead parrotfish frolic in the upper reaches, munching coral and spewing sand.

Tunicates pumping on the Cherry Blossom Wall.

53 Sunrise Reef

This is one of Yap's showplaces for hard coral growth. While not necessarily blessed with an abundance of fish, the coral formations take on pretzel-like twists and turns where competition for space has been intense. Just about every variety of Micronesian hard coral sits here.

Location: Northeast coast
Depth Range: 20-80 ft (6-24 meters)
Access: Boat
Expertise Rating: Novice

The gradual slope has left the corals well-protected most of the year and provides room for the reef to expand. Look for the large coral heads that pop up from the reef. If you peer closely you'll see that the heads provide habitat to fish and Christmas tree worms in dozens of hues and color combinations.

This is also a good place to look for mottled stingrays and bull rays in the deeper reaches. Giant clams like this habitat, as do small hawksbill turtles.

Christmas tree worm.

54 Goofnuw Mini Wall

This large wall faces the open sea along the south side of Goofnuw Channel, so expect to see many different creatures than normally found on the hard coral reefs. This is a good place to see a leopard shark resting in the center of the channel or swimming in and out of the many coral heads along the bottom.

Location: Goofnuw Channel
Depth Range: 20-80 ft (6-24 meters)
Access: Boat
Expertise Rating: Intermediate

Large stingrays like this habitat, so look closely as they may be buried in the white sand that accumulates near the brain corals. Schools of snappers and bumphead parrotfish course in and out of this channel and mantas can be seen entering the mouth as they come in for feeding or cleaning.

This mouth is the spillway for large volumes of water, so a drift dive at incoming tide can be a real rocket ride into the cleaning stations. It is possible to duck the current to look around the corals by hiding beneath a big bommie (coral head). When you're finished looking, just expose yourself to the current again and away you go!

TIM ROCK

Stingrays like the sandy floor at Goofnuw Mini Wall.

55 Goofnuw Channel

Although Miil Channel is usually associated with manta rays, in June through October mantas are more likely to be found in greater profusion in Goofnuw Channel.

Studies show that the mantas migrate to Goofnuw in the summer and are found in as great concentrations as in Miil the rest of the year.

Unlike the ridge at Miil, Goofnuw has a mound that rises to about 40 ft. Currents flow around large coral heads and over the mound, providing a good feeding spot for the mantas.

Each of these various coral heads are cleaning stations and have been given a

Location: Northeast Yap
Depth Range: 20-80 ft (6-24 meters)
Access: Boat
Expertise Rating: Novice

TIM ROCK

Manta rays come to Goofnuw in the summer.

site nickname like Merry-Go-Round, Manta Rock and Car Wash. They are all close to one another and can be explored in one dive. Just down the channel there is also a cleaning station at about 35 ft along the northern wall. The white, reflective sand makes this site excellent for photography.

The rest of this channel is good to dive as well, and again, it is best at slack, high tide to get optimum visibility, which is about 60 to 80 ft.

Sometimes moray eels seem to poke out from every hole. Hawksbill turtles and whitetip sharks rest on the bottom, too. There are various hard corals, especially on the coral heads in the channel center. Juvenile fish also like this habitat.

TIM ROCK

Hard corals dotted with tunicates and ascidians.

56 Shark City

Farther up the channel is Shark City, named for all of the whitetip sharks found resting on the sandy bottom. This spot begins with powdery white sand. Divers can swim from here to the main cleaning stations in the channel, seeing varied terrain and, normally, a lot of sharks.

There is also a chance to see a "pack" of grey reef sharks in the area. Especially during the summer months, groups of 5 to 8 greys will patrol Shark City and the cleaning stations. This may be a mating activity, as the rest of the year there is usually just one territorial grey seen in the vicinity.

Location: Goofnuw Channel
Depth Range: 15-60 ft (5-18 meters)
Access: Boat
Expertise Rating: Novice

Look for large pufferfish sleeping in the middle of the channel during the day. Shells and other invertebrates can also be found if you take this dive easy and aren't in too big of a rush to get to the mantas.

57 Garden Eel Flats

Location: Miil Channel
Depth Range: 20-95 ft (6-29 meters)
Access: Boat
Expertise Rating: Intermediate

Far up the Miil Channel, east of the mooring buoys at the cleaning station and toward the islands, is a good sandy bar in which to watch the many sea creatures move through the channel.

You'll find this site on the right side of the channel as you face the sea. Divers normally swim at 40 to 60 ft here, observing coral and whatever fish swim up the channel. Soon you'll arrive at a long, sloping bank covered with tons of red and golden gorgonians. The sandslide starts in about 25 ft and cascades down past 70 ft. The gorgonians have snowy, white polyps and thrive on the plankton sweeping through the channel that spills into Miil.

Down the sloping wall at 70 ft, white sand falls into the channel, forming a landscaped plain with corals, fans and small baitfish. Observant divers will see the garden of small eels. These animals live individually in burrows from which they pop out to feed on plankton. From a distance, they might look like a carpet of sea grass swaying in the breeze. It is easy to miss them as they completely disappear if alarmed. They don't like bubbles, so take shallow breaths and exhale slowly.

This is a great spot for macro or wide angle work, as lots of fish visit the area. An ancient stone money piece is also in the channel, although how it got there is unknown. Check out the individual large bumphead parrotfish, lots of small baitfish on branching corals and even an occasional turtle. Eagle rays also come by and sea anemones abound here. Green cup coral stands thrive in the channel current. Also, keep an eye out for solitary large snappers.

TIM ROCK

A manta swims over a stone money piece, thrown into channel during WWII to prevent its destruction.

58 Manta Cleaning Station

This is a relatively new site the mantas have been visiting in recent years. It is shallow along the upper shelf so you can log lots of time observing the rays. When the water is clear at early high tide, snorkelers can usually enjoy a manta sighting too.

Just find a spot near the cleaning station and wait for the parade to begin. The mantas travel up and down the channel so keep a lookout into the wide channel flats. Mantas swoop in individually or in pairs to partake in the cleaning action.

Nearby you'll find a sea anemone with dusky clownfish, some large cup coral trees, star coral heads and a nice coral garden. Here crocodilefish like to stealthily sit and wait for prey. Look for them among the open blossoms of the flower corals.

Location: Miil Channel

Depth Range: 20-90 ft (6-27 meters)

Access: Boat

Expertise Rating: Novice

Camouflaged crocodilefish are found all along the reef top at Miil Channel.

Small fish pick parasites off the mantas at Manta Cleaning Station.

Photographing Mantas

Those familiar with shipwreck photography will find some of the same challenges when photographing mantas. Mantas reside in these channels because the waters are rich in nutrients, which is great for mantas but not so swell for photographers. Just as silt causes backscatter problems on shipwrecks, the planktonic matter in the channels is also highly reflective.

The second problem is the animals themselves. Their backs are normally dark gray to black, while their undersides are snow white. To bring out their natural colors without making their bellies shine like the moon and their surroundings appear to be stars in the sky, I suggest you power down.

Shooting with the strobe at one-half power or even one-quarter power is quite helpful as it reduces the scatter problem and fills in the white of the belly to give a nice, natural appearance. It also doesn't take as long to recycle, which is important as the mantas do come close, but they don't always stay for long.

Also, stay put and breath easy. The mantas will simply disappear if chased or touched. You can virtually kiss your manta shooting goodbye if you start swimming after them. They are curious and will come your way sooner or later. Also, while they do not seem to be particularly annoyed by bubbles, a slow, controlled exhalation will keep them around longer.

As the animals do tend to get very close at times (I've had one fill the frame of a 16mm full-frame fisheye), the choice of lens is really up to you. If you want to get some of the reef's corals or fish life in the foreground and have the mantas in the mid-ground, use your wide angle; 20mm to 50mm is an appropriate lens

range for fish and large animal shots. Film choice again depends on the effect you want to create, but 100 ASA will give you needed depth of field and shutter speed, while still keeping the grain down. On sunny days, the lighting can be quite good. On cloudy days, the nutrients help soak up the light, so even at 30 ft, it can mean dark water.

For video, remember, the picture is supposed to be moving, not the camera. Let the animals swim to the camera and in and out of frame for the best editing advantages. If you must move the camera, remember to pan with the action. In other words, follow the animal. Don't even touch the zoom button. Underwater zooms are rarely effective.

59 Manta Ridge

This site is virtually guaranteed to provide high voltage diving action. Manta Ridge got its name because divers can just about be assured of seeing a manta when diving along this ridge. Dived usually at tide change when the high tide is incoming or slack, the site is a rise in the 90 ft-deep channel. This small pinnacle comes up to about 33 ft and the current sweeps over the top. Divers need merely to hang on to a rock and wait to see what the current will bring.

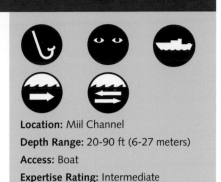

Location: Miil Channel
Depth Range: 20-90 ft (6-27 meters)
Access: Boat
Expertise Rating: Intermediate

A school of crevalle jacks constantly circles the region, while sharks slide in and out of view, swimming close to stationary divers. Red, black and white snappers hang in loose schools at the base of the pinnacle and sea whips flow with the current. On the channel side, a garden of bright red soft corals blossoms and seems to grow larger every year.

The manta experience is the true clincher, however. One moment, you're looking into a murky abyss and the next moment, here they come! Gracefully coursing through the water, a full-grown manta will glide into view, swoop overhead and linger there with you for what seems like forever. Then the manta will wing away, soaring into the sun and out of sight.

There is a gorgeous anemone here with shocking purple tips and skunk clownfish. Green moray eels are found in some of the holes on the ridge. The relatively shallow depth allows for a lot of bottom time.

Soft red corals abound on the wall along the Ridge.

60 Miil Point

Some divers prefer to take a short swim up the channel before carrying on to the Manta Ridge. The boat can drop you off at a fork in the channel, where there is a nice wall covered with lots of hard coral. It is common to see eagle rays out in the blue expanse. Whitetip sharks sleep on the bottom. One group saw a shark with a fin missing and, judging from the crescent shape of the bite, there is apparently no honor or professional courtesy among sharks. Small eels poke from holes and stunning spotted groupers are so unafraid of divers they will not move away if gently observed. Jacks can be very cooperative on some days, allowing close approach and

Location: Miil Channel

Depth Range: 30-90 ft (9-27 meters)

Access: Boat

Expertise Rating: Intermediate

even a swim through the school. Look for the garden of soft red corals in the valley.

After your short swim, settle down and wait for the mantas that come to Manta Ridge, or carry on to the Manta Cleaning Station.

Mating Mantas

From December through mid-April, one of nature's most fantastic displays takes place when the mantas perform mating rituals. In the distance you can see them coming, swimming in formations one after another, performing incredible aquabatics in a follow-the-leader style.

The males flip, spin, turn and twist in an attempt to gain the eye and favor of a female, who does the same actions to entice or avoid a suitor. Sometimes oblivious to the diver, they will continue this show for quite a long time, moving up and down the channel. Often they will perform near the surface, darting through the sunlight that filters down. If you have the opportunity to travel to Yap during mating season, don't miss the chance to make some channel dives. There is a good chance you can observe this wild behavior.

STEPHANIE BRENDL

61 Spaghetti Factory

Diving in Miil Channel has traditionally been the domain of manta ray watchers, but there is more to see for those who care to take a swim. The channel mouth provides the opportunity to see lots of other fish as well.

Location: Miil Channel
Depth Range: 20-130 ft (6-40 meters)
Access: Boat
Expertise Rating: Advanced

Currents flowing from the mangroves to the sea carry sediments, organic debris and drifting sea life. This provides a rich food source for the mantas, but is for visibility. The best time to dive here is at high slack tide, which means clearer water, little or no current and easier swimming.

After a short swim up the left side of the wall, a slope appears, covered with a veritable garden of sea whips that look something like spaghetti. It was at the Spaghetti Factory that a dive group saw a giant manta—a good 14 ft wingspan—casually swim by before taking off up the channel. Divers also report seeing eagle rays and sharks along the bottom.

Nearby is a cleaning station frequented by grey reef sharks. Ask your guide to show you this spot so you can watch a grey having its dentures done.

Noodle-like whip corals along the wall at the Spaghetti Factory.

62 Manta Ray Bay

The Yap Divers boat will drop divers at the steep wall near the outer reef. Here the walls drop almost vertically and are covered with large plate corals. The rocky outcrops that occasionally pop out of the wall are prime sites for immense gorgonians in many hues, including brilliant yellows. There are lots of beautiful hydroids too, but they can leave a nasty sting so be careful.

Location: Northeast Yap
Depth Range: 20-80 ft (6-24 meters)
Access: Boat
Expertise Rating: Intermediate

While Miil generally averages about 90 ft visibility, it is a good 140 ft here and the clarity can be deceiving. Keep a close eye on your depth gauge and computer.

A large point doglegs in the channel and is a good spot to swim across to the right side in order not to miss the ridge, as there is a deceiving fork farther up the channel.

It can be a unique, humbling trip across the blue void as one side of the channel wall disappears before the other can be seen. Take caution as the channel is wide and deep. The right side is full of anemones and many make great close-up subjects. Schools of pyramid butterflyfish coast up and down the wall and provide lots of golden color. Bumphead parrotfish graze up in the shallows and there are also lots of Moorish idols.

The end of the dive can be spent observing the schools of jacks, snappers and drum and the bonus manta at the ridge. This is an excellent way to see the terrain of a mangrove channel that empties into sea. The size of the sheer walls and broad channel basin truly dwarf the diver, who gains an appreciation for the volume of water that moves through this unique ecosystem.

Daisy corals on the outer reef.

Yellow gorgonians grow on rocky outcrops.

Marine Life

The creatures pictured here are just a sampling of the marine life found around Guam, Rota and Yap. The highly diverse ecosystems are full of a wide variety of fish and invertebrates. The range of hard corals in these Western Pacific waters make the diving fascinating, and the reef life abundant and full.

The names immediately below the photographs represent the common names, as they are used most frequently on the islands. The second name indicates the scientific classification of the family (F), class (Cl) or phylum (Ph).

Common Fishes

blue face angelfish
F. *Pomacanthidae*

emperor angelfish
F. *Pomacanthidae*

threadfin butterflyfish
F. *Chaetodontidae*

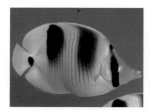
double saddle butterflyfish
F. *Chaetodontidae*

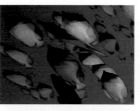
pyramid butterflyfish
F. *Chaetodontidae*

trumpetfish
F. *Aulostomidae*

chromis
F. *Pomacentridae*

"buffalo" parrotfish
F. *Scaridae*

stoplight parrotfish
F. *Scaridae*

batfish (spadefish)
F. *Ephippidae*

dusky clownfish
F. *Pomacentridae*

skunk clownfish
F. *Pomacentridae*

two-stripe anemonefish
F. *Pomacentridae*

Clark's anemonefish
F. *Pomacentridae*

surgeonfish
F. *Acanthuridae*

pufferfish
F. *Tetraodontidae*

spiny pufferfish
F. *Tetraodontidae*

goatfish
F. *Mullidae*

blenny
F. *Blennidae*

anthias
F. *Serranidae*

needlefish
F. *Belonidae*

Invertebrates

tridacna clam
Cl. *Pelycypoda*

cleaner shrimp
Cl. *Malacostraca*

commensal shrimp
Cl. *Malacostraca*

mat anemone
Cl. *Anthozoa*

carpet anemone
Cl. *Anthozoa*

anemone crab
Cl. *Malacostraca*

hermit crab
Cl. *Malacostraca*

tunicates
Cl. *Ascidiacea*

ascidians
Cl. *Ascidiacea*

tube sponge
Ph. *Porifera*

barrel sponge
Ph. *Porifera*

branching coral
Cl. *Anthozoa*

tube corals
Cl. *Anthozoa*

sea fans
Cl. *Anthozoa*

sea whips
Cl. *Anthozoa*

Unusual Fish & Invertebrates

bonnetshell
Cl. *Gastropoda*

crocodilefish
F. *Platycephalidae*

sand anemone
Cl. *Anthozoa*

leaf scorpionfish
F. *Scorpaenidae*

pipefish
F. *Syngnathidae*

pizza nudibranch
Cl. *Gastropoda*

Hazardous Marine Life

Just as there are bears, bees and poison ivy in the forest, the ocean has its share of natural hazards. Respect the marine creatures listed below to minimize the potential for an unpleasant encounter. Some of the common remedies are listed, but always consult a physician in the event of an ocean–related injury.

Fire Coral You will find these stingers in all Micronesian waters, but more heavily present in Yap's prolific channels. Fire coral looks like small ferns, and turtles like to eat it. Humans, however, can get a nasty sting when the nema-

tocysts (small stinging cells on the polyps) discharge, causing a burning sensation that lasts for several minutes and can cause red welts on the skin. If you brush against fire coral, do not try to rub the area as you will spread the stinging particles.

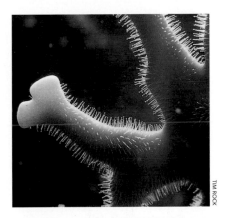

Stings should be treated with vinegar. An antihistamine cream is good for killing the pain. Application of a local anesthetic may also be necessary for some people.

Jellyfish & Stinging Drifters

The waters of Guam, Yap and Rota generally have no strongly toxic jellyfish. Small jellyfish—especially the *Mastigias spp.*—are common. Stings are often irritating but not painful. As rule, the longer the jellyfish's tentacles, the more painful the sting. Some people may have an unusually strong reaction to certain jellyfish toxins.

A far more dangerous visitor to these waters is the Portuguese Man-o-War, sometimes called Blue Bonnets. These colonial organisms

The Portuguese Man-o-War is extremely toxic, even when it is washed up on the beach and appears to be dead.

(distant cousins of the jellyfish) are most common around inshore reefs from September through November. They may be spotted from the surface by their brilliant blue "floats" that serve to suspend their body mass. The long, trailing tentacles are armed with exceedingly toxic and painful stinging cells. Give these animals a wide berth, as the cells are capable of discharge even when the tentacle has completely broken off the body or when the creature is washed up on shore and appears lifeless. If stung, apply vinegar or ammonia and get to a physician quickly.

Cone Shells Viewing and photographing shells in the islands is a favorite pastime of many macrophotographers. But, as a rule of thumb, look but don't touch. Cone shells can be a serious, very toxic, health hazard. Avoid picking them up as they attack their prey by shooting a tiny poison dart from their funnel-like

proboscis. The stung area will go numb, and can be followed by muscular paralysis, respiratory paralysis and even, in extreme cases, heart failure. Apply a broad ligature between the wound and body, be prepared to use CPR and get the victim to a hospital quickly.

Triggerfish When you see the variety and size of triggerfish in these islands, their appearance on this list doesn't seem so amusing. At Guam's Ypao Beach, panicked tourists reacting to nips from tiny Picasso triggerfish are the greatest cause of lifeguard rescue. Bites from the larger mustache triggerfish can draw blood. If a fish chases you, avoid its nesting area and move on quickly. Treat bites with antiseptics, anti-tetanus and antibiotics.

Venomous Creatures

Venomous sea creatures include fish, invertebrates and shells. In these waters watch out for **scorpionfish** and **lionfish**, whose razor-sharp spines can go through gloves, booties and even fins. Wounds can cause intense pain. (Fish stings result mostly from people wading on or placing an inadvertent hand or arm on, say, a scorpionfish.) Also look out for the **crown-of-thorns starfish**. These creatures can deliver a painful sting even if they've been dead for two to three days.

For stings, soak in warm water for at least 2 hours. Apply a broad ligature between the sting and the body, releasing it every 15 minutes. Do this until the pain subsides. A local anesthetic also helps. Seek medical care.

Scorpionfish

Lionfish

Crown-of-thorns starfish

Moray eel

Eels Moray eels are common on these reefs. Normally, eels are shy and retreat upon seeing a diver. You're only likely to get bitten if you put your hands in holes or crevices. Morays have sharp teeth that slant backward in their mouths. If you are bitten, don't pull back immediately to avoid nasty tears to the skin and muscle tissue. Treat with antiseptics, anti-tetanus and antibiotics.

TIM ROCK

Barracuda These fish rarely attack divers, but it has been known to happen. One case occurred on Guam when a great barracuda thought to be tame was being hand fed. The fish got a portion of thumb and the hand needed reconstructive surgery. They occasionally bite if they get confused by a flashing object in turbid water. Like morays, barracudas can hang on. Treat as you would a moray bite.

Sharks Sharks are found in the deeper waters of Guam and occur more frequently at dive sites in Yap and Rota. The most common are grey reef sharks and whitetips, both of which are not normally aggressive toward divers. Virtually all shark attacks in the islands happen in conjunction with spearfishing. Don't spearfish and your likelihood of attack is greatly decreased. If a shark does bite, treat the victim for both the cut and shock. In severe cases, stop the bleeding by applying pressure or a tourniquet. The victim should be transported to the hospital. Minor slashes should be treated with an antibacterial and a tetanus preventative.

TIM ROCK

Diving Conservation & Awareness

TIM ROCK

Reef Etiquette

Dive sites tend to be located where the reefs and walls display the most beautiful corals and sponges. It only takes a moment—an inadvertently placed hand or knee on the coral or an unaware brush or kick with a fin—to destroy this fragile, living part of our delicate ecosystem. Please consider the following tips when diving and help preserve the ecology and beauty of the reefs:

1. Maintain proper buoyancy control and avoid over-weighting. Be aware that buoyancy can change over the period of an extended trip: initially you may breathe harder and need more weighting; a few days later you may breath more easily and need less weight.

2. Use correct weight belt position to stay horizontal, i.e., raise the belt above your waist to elevate your feet/fins, and move it lower toward your hips to lower them.

Keeping the Mantas Wild

TIM ROCK

Yap dive operators want to keep the mantas wild, allowing them to exist in their natural setting while being observed by divers. Altering the natural behavior of the mantas could be disastrous for the small, obliging family that has become such a worldwide attraction. Any action that might cause the animals to let down their natural defenses, become injured or become dependent on humans is not a favorable move for the mantas. Thus, visiting divers are asked to not attempt to ride, touch or chase the animals. Fish feeding is also not done here. Not only does it upset the natural eating habits of the mantas, but it also attracts the many predators always lurking nearby.

3. Use your tank position in the backpack as a balance weight, i.e., raise your backpack on the tank to lower your legs, and lower the backpack on the tank to raise your legs.

4. Be careful about buoyancy loss at depth; the deeper you go the more your wetsuit compresses, and the more buoyancy you lose.

5. Photographers must be extra careful. Cameras and equipment affect buoyancy. Changing f-stops, framing a subject, and maintaining position for a photo often conspire to prohibit the ideal "no-touch" approach on a reef. So, when you must use "holdfasts," choose them intelligently (i.e., use one finger only for leverage off an area of dead coral).

6. Avoid full leg kicks when working close to the bottom and when leaving a photo scene. When you inadvertently kick something, stop kicking! Seems obvious, but some divers either semi-panic or are totally oblivious when they bump something. When treading water in shallow reef areas, take care not to kick up clouds of sand. Settling sand can easily smother the delicate organisms of the reef.

Marine Conservation Organizations

Coral reefs and oceans are facing unprecedented environmental pressures. The following groups are actively involved in promoting responsible diving practices, publicizing environmental marine threats, and lobbying for better policies.

Project AWARE Foundation
Tel: 714-540-0251
www.projectaware.org

CORAL: The Coral Reef Alliance
Tel: 510-848-0110
www.coral.org/

Coral Forest
Tel: 415-788-REEF; www.blacktop.com/coralforest/

Cousteau Society
Tel: 757-523-9335
www.cousteau.org

Ocean Futures
Tel: 714-456-0790
www.oceanfutures.org

ReefKeeper International
Tel: 305-358-4600
www.reefkeeper.org

7. When swimming in strong currents, be extra careful about leg kicks and handholds.

8. Attach dangling gauges, computer consoles, and octopus regulators. They are like miniature wrecking balls to a reef.

9. Never drop boat anchors onto a coral reef, and take care not to ground boats on coral. Encourage dive operators and regulatory bodies to establish permanent moorings at popular dive sites.

10. Resist the temptation to collect or buy corals or shells. Aside from the ecological damage, taking home marine souvenirs depletes the beauty of a site and spoils the enjoyment of others.

11. Resist the temptation to feed fish. You may disturb their normal eating habits, encourage aggressive behavior, or feed them food that is detrimental to their health.

Listings

To call Guam, Rota or Yap, dial your international access code for the country you are calling from (in the U.S. it's 011) + the area code and local 7-digit number. The area code for Guam is (671), Rota (670) and Yap (691).

Accommodations

Guam

Fujita Guam Tumon Beach Hotel
(283 rooms, 3 suites)
153 Fujita Road & Pale San Vitores Road
Tumon, Guam 96911
☎ 646-1811 Fax: 646-1605
Western and Japanese restaurants, 2 swimming pools, jacuzzi, karaoke rooms, gift shops, medical services, laundry, ocean view.

Guam Airport Hotel
(51 rooms, 3 suites)
P.O. Box 10239
Tamuning, Guam 96931
☎ 649-8402 Fax: 649-8401
Continental restaurant, swimming pool, laundry.

Guam Garden Villa
(3 rooms)
P.O. Box 10167
Sinajania, Guam 96926
☎ 477-8166
Bed & Breakfast, continental breakfast.

Guam Hilton Hotel
(691 rooms, 26 suites)
P.O. Box 11199
Tamuning, Guam 96932
☎ 646-1835 Fax: 646-1190
Continental, Japanese, European and Asian restaurants, coffee house, outdoor lounge, swimming pool, various water sports activities, fitness center, beach club, tennis courts, conference rooms, shopping arcade.

Harmon Loop Hotel
(62 rooms)
1900 Harmon Loop Road
Suite 107
Dededo, Guam 96912
☎ 632-3353 Fax: 632-3330
Restaurant next door, lobby coffee service, air conditioning, cable TV.

Hotel Sunroute Guam
(71 rooms)
1433 Pale San Vitores Road
Tumon, Guam 96911
☎ 649-9670 Fax: 649-0562
Chamorro restaurant, swimming pool, boutique, view of Agana Bay.

Hyatt Regency Guam
(455 rooms, 19 suites)
1155 Pale San Vitores Road
Tumon, Guam 96911
☎ 647-1234 Fax: 647-1235
Japanese, Italian, international, and Mexican restaurants, business center, conference and banquet rooms, art gallery, fitness center, swimming pools, water park, shopping.

Inn on the Bay
(70 rooms, 62 suites)
P.O. Box 83900
Agat, Guam 96928
☎ 565- 8521 Fax: 565-8527
iotb@ite.net
Caters to divers and has a package with PSD. Restaurant, swimming pool, on-site bank, pharmacy, rental cars, southern ocean view, shopping arcade.

Outrigger Guam Resort
(600 rooms)
1255 Pale San Vitores Road
Tumon, Guam 96911
☎ 649-9000 Fax: 649-9068
Pool, restaurant, lounge, water sports center, fitness center, spa, banquet facilities.

Pacific Islands Club
(501 rooms, 3 suites)
P.O. Box 9370
Tamuning, Guam 96931
☎ 646-9171 Fax: 646-5762
Scuba and snorkeling intros and a full-size indoor aquarium for snorkeling. Continental, Chinese, Western, and Japanese restaurants, coffee house, disco. 5 swimming pools, water park, putter golf, in-line skate park, tennis, racquetball, and squash courts, club type activities, shopping arcade.

Tamuning Plaza Hotel
(66 rooms, 20 suites)
960 South Marine Drive
Tamuning, Guam 96931
☎ 649-8646 Fax: 649-8651
American restaurant and bar.

Westin Resort Guam
(420 rooms)
105 Gun Beach Road
Tumon, Guam 96911
☎ 647-1020 Fax: 646-0931
Chinese, Italian, Japanese restaurants, coffee shop, swimming pool, shopping arcade, meeting rooms.

Rota

Bay View Hotel
(9 rooms)
P.O. Box 875
Rota, MP 96951
☎ 532-3414 Fax: 532-0393
Airport transfer, laundry service,
restaurant, room service.

Blue Peninsula Inn
(14 rooms)
Rota, MP 96951
☎ 532-0468 Fax: 532-0841
Airport transfer, room service,
laundry service, restaurant, bar.

Coconut Village
(20 rooms)
P.O. Box 855
Rota, MP 96951
☎ 834-5511 Fax: 834-5512
Airport transfer, swimming
pool, bar, restaurant, tour
desk, gift shop.

Coral Garden Hotel
(18 rooms)
P.O. Box 597

Rota, MP 96951
☎ 532-3201 Fax: 532-3204
Airport transfer, room service,
laundry service.

Figueroa's
(4 rooms)
P.O. Box 1524
Rota, MP 96951
☎ 532-1337 Fax: 532-1338
Airport transfer, restaurant,
bar, guest lounge.

Jotina Inn
(10 rooms)
P.O. Box 887
Rota, MP 96951
☎ 532-0500/0499/0392
Fax: 532-0703
Airport transfer, room service,
tour desk, mini-mart, deli.

Rota Hotel
(30 rooms)
P.O. Box 878
Rota, MP 96951
☎ 532-2000 Fax: 532-3000

Airport transfer, restaurant,
bar, swimming pool, tour desk,
gift/sundry, shop, bicycle, golf
club and marine & beach
equipment rental, mini-bar,
BBQ dinner, currency
exchange, room service.

Rota Pau Pau Hotel
(20 rooms)
P.O. Box 855
Rota, MP 96951
☎ 834-5511 Fax: 834-5512
Airport transfer, pool, bar,
restaurant, tour desk, gift shop.

Rota Resort & Country Club
(20 rooms)
P.O. Box 938
Rota, MP 96951
☎ 532-1155 Fax: 532-1156
rota.manager@saipan.com
Airport transfer, pool, bar,
restaurant, tour desk,
gift shop.

Yap

Destiny Hotel
P.O. Box 428, Yap, FSM 96943
☎ 350-4188 Fax: 350-4187

ESA Hotel
P.O. Box 141, Yap, FSM 96943
☎ 350-2139 Fax: 350-2310

Manta Ray Bay Hotel
P.O. Box MR, Yap, FSM 96943
☎ 350-2300 Fax: 350-4567
yapdivers@mantaray.com

Ocean View Hotel
P.O. Box 130, Yap, FSM 96943
☎ 350-3106 Fax: 350-2339

Pathways Hotel
P.O. Box 718, Yap, FSM 96943
☎ 350-3310 Fax: 350-2066
pathways@mail.fm

Village View Hotel
P.O. Box 611 Yap, FSM 96943
☎ 350-3956 Fax: 350-3956
villageview@mail.fm

Dining

Guam

Fine Dining

Al Dente
Hyatt Regency Guam
☎ 647-1234

Claret
Guam Dai Ichi Hotel
☎ 646-5881

Creations
Pacific Star Hotel
☎ 649-7827

Islands Fisherman Restaurant
Tamuning
☎ 646-6971

Roy's Restaurant
Guam Hilton
☎ 646-1835

Continental Dining

Cafe Sirena
Pacific Star Hotel
☎ 649-7827

Chuck's Steakhouse
Upper Tumon
☎ 646-1001

Island Terrace
Guam Hilton
☎ 646-1835

La Mirenda
Hyatt Regency Guam
☎ 647-1234

Outback Steakhouse
Tumon
☎ 646-1543

Planet Hollywood
Tumon
☎ 647-7827

Chinese
China House
Guam Dai Ichi Hotel
☎ 646-5881

Ocean City Restaurant
Tamuning
☎ 649-8795

Sam Wo Chinese Restaurant
Tumon
☎ 646-8268

Japanese
Benkay Restaurant
Hotel Nikko Guam
☎ 649-8815

Genji Restaurant
Guam Hilton
☎ 646-1835

Inaka Sushi Bar
Sotetsu Tropicana Hotel
☎ 646-5851

Issin Japanese Teppan Yaki & Sushi
Westin Resort
☎ 647-1020

Niji
Hyatt Regency Guam
☎ 647-1234

Casual Dining
Chamoru-Tei Restaurant
Hotel Sunroute Guam
☎ 649-9670

Denny's
Inn on the Bay
☎ 565-8521

Jeff's Pirates Cove
Ipan
☎ 789-2683

Little Caesar's
Kmart
☎ 649-9878

Lone Star Steaks
Tamuning
☎ 649-3497

Micronesia Mall Fiesta Court
Micronesia Mall
☎ 632-8881

Sizzler
Agana
☎ 649-3497

Tony Roma's
Tamuning
☎ 646-9034

Rota

As Pari's Restaurant
Songsong Village
☎ 532-3356

Bay Breeze Snack Bar
Across from Dive Rota
☎ 532-7575

Chamoru Restaurant
Songsong Village
☎ 532-2233

Cool Spot
Songsong Village
☎ 532-3414

Del Mar Restaurant
Rota Hotel
☎ 532-2000

Figueroa's
Songsong Village
☎ 532-2337

Hibiscus Restaurant
Coconut Village Hotel
☎ 532-3448

Pacifica Restaurant
Rota Resort
☎ 532-1155

Plumeria Restaurant
Pau Pau Hotel
☎ 532-3561

Tokyo-En Restaurant
Songsong Village
☎ 532-1266

Tonga Tonga Cafe
Songsong Village
☎ 532-1010

Yap

Restaurants
ESA Restaurant
☎ 350-2138

Kool Korner
YMCA Complex,
Second Floor
☎ 350-2460

Manta Ray Bar & Grill
Manta Ray Bay Hotel
☎ 350-2300

Marina Restaurant
☎ 350-2211

Oceanview Restaurant
☎ 350-2279

Pathways Restaurant
Pathways Hotel
☎ 350-3310

Sakura Kai Restaurant
Next to O'Keefe's
☎ 350-3880

Bars
Marina Bar
Yap Marina

Nautical Weaver Bar
Manta Ray Bay Hotel

O'Keefe's Tavern
Adjacent to Sakura Kai

Pathways Bar
Pathways Hotel

Diving Services

Guam

Aquatic Tours

P.O. Box 24849
Tamuning, Guam 96933
☎ 646-1696 Fax: 646-1620

Sales & Rentals:	Sales of various name brands; rentals available with tours
Air:	On-site compressor
Credit Cards:	All major credit cards accepted
Boats:	2 boats operate daily
Trips:	Daily trips to neighboring islands: Palau, Yap, Truk Lagoon, etc.
Courses:	3-day open water course, advanced
Other:	Divers can plan their own itineraries

Fish Eye Diving Guam, Inc.

900 North Marine Drive
Piti, Guam 96925
☎ 475-7000 Fax: 477-2550

Sales & Rentals:	Sales of name brands; rentals available with tours
Air:	On-site compressor
Credit Cards:	All major credit cards accepted
Boats:	1 boat operates daily
Trips:	Southern Guam and unique sites such as 11-Mile Reef
Courses:	PADI certification
Other:	Daily intro dives to the marine observatory. On-site freshwater pool for training. English and Japanese speaking divemasters

Gently Blue

Holiday Plaza Hotel #2103
Tumon, Guam 96925
☎ 646-0838 Fax: 646-0838

Email:	aki@ite.net
Website:	www.pluto.dti.ne.jp/~marvin/
Sales & Rentals:	Full scuba equipment for rent or sale
Credit Cards:	All major credit cards accepted
Boats:	Custom dive boat, 28 ft
Trips:	Trips to all local dive sites
Courses:	PADI open water to divemaster & 11 specialty courses
Other:	PADI 5-star facility

Guam Tropical Dive Station

P.O. Box 1649
Agana, Guam 96932
☎ 477-2774 Fax: 477-2775

Email:	gtds@ite.net
Website:	www.gtds.com
Sales & Rentals:	Full range of scuba equipment; sales include cameras & underwater communication equipment
Credit Cards:	All major credit cards accepted
Air:	Nitrox, mixed gas & oxygen fills available
Boats:	3 boats: 18 ft (6 passengers), 24 ft (12 passengers), 42 ft (40 passengers)
Trips:	Daily trips including night dives
Courses:	PADI open water to instructor
Other:	5-star IDC facility, open 7 days/week

Micronesian Divers Association, Inc.

856 North Marine Drive
Piti, Guam 96925
☎ 472-6321 Fax: 477-6329

Email:	mda@mdaguam.com
Website:	www.mdaguam.com
Sales & Rentals:	Full scuba equipment for rent or sale
Credit Cards:	All major credit cards accepted
Air:	Nitrox & oxygen fills available
Boats:	2 modern 42 ft dive boats designed for diving
Trips:	Daily trips to more than 50 sites, from the northern tip and east side to everything in between
Courses:	Weekly classes; PADI open water & specialty classes to instructor
Other:	Largest dive operation in Western Pacific; PADI 5-star IDC facility; fully certified repair department

Papalagi Diving

901-C Pale San Vitores Road
Tumon, Guam 96911
☎ 649-3483 Fax: 649-3498

Sales & Rentals:	Sales of top name brands, rentals available
Credit Cards:	All major credit cards accepted
Air:	On-site compressor
Boats:	Boats operating daily
Trips:	Daily trips to popular Guam sites
Courses:	PADI open water to divemaster
Other:	Japanese speaking a specialty

Professional Sports Divers

P.O. Box 8630
Agat, Guam 96928
☎ 565-3488 Fax: 565-3633

Email:	psdivers@kuentos.guam.net
Website:	www.psdguam.com
Sales & Rentals:	Full range of scuba equipment for recreational & technical diving
Credit Cards:	All Major credit cards accepted
Air:	Nitrox, timix, heliox & oxygen fills available
Boats:	*Sportdiver* (6-cabin cruiser), *Pegasus* (power catamaran, holds 15 divers & 30 tanks)
Trips:	Daily boat dives, kayak trips, live-aboard arrangements
Courses:	All PADI & NAUI courses; IANTD recreational, technical & instructor training; British Sub Aqua School
Other:	Hotel packages, airport & hotel pick-ups

Rainbow Dolphin & Diving

P.O. Box 10417
Tamuning, Guam 96925
☎ 646-6743 Fax: 646-6743

Email:	rainbow@kuentos.guam.net
Sales & Rentals:	Full scuba rentals
Credit Cards:	All major credit cards accepted
Air:	Nitrox & oxygen fills available
Boats:	*Rainbow Runner* (16 divers) & *Rainbow Chaser* (16 divers)
Trips:	Trips to all local dive sites
Courses:	NAUI & PADI open water to instructor
Other:	Dolphin-watching and snorkeling tours also available

Real World Diving Company

P.O. Box 2800
Agana, Guam 96932

☎ 646-8903 Fax: 646-4957

Email:	rwdolphin@ite.net
Website:	www.rwdiving.com
Sales & Rentals:	Most scuba equipment for rent or sale, including lights
Credit Cards:	All major credit cards accepted
Air:	Nitrox, mixed gas & oxygen fills available
Boats:	*Toninos* (40 divers), *Real World II* (19 divers), *Umibuta* (21 divers), *Real World I* (6 divers)
Trips:	Feature north side and offshore dive trips
Courses:	PADI open water to divemaster, PADI, SSI referral courses
Other:	Private boat charters from 4–40 divers

Scuba Company

221 Farenholt Ave., Suite 101
Tamuning, Guam 96933
☎ 649-3369 Fax: 649-3379

Email:	scubaco@ite.net
Sales & Rentals:	Full service dive shop with top brands for sale. Factory-trained equipment repair specialists, full rentals
Air:	Two on-site compressors
Credit Cards:	All major credit cards accepted
Boats:	*Andromeda Pro 48* (35 divers), *Andromeda 42* (25 divers)
Trips:	Daily trips including northern Guam
Courses:	PADI open water to divemaster courses in English and Japanese
Other:	PADI 5-star facility; daily dolphin tours

Rota

Dive Rota

P.O. Box 941
Rota, MP 95951
☎ 532-3377 Fax: 532-3022

Sales & Rentals:	Most scuba equipment for sale; equipment & camera rentals
Credit Cards:	Most major credit cards accepted
Air:	Oxygen fills available; 2 on-site compressors
Boats:	*Asakaze* (5 divers), *Akebono* (6 divers)
Trips:	Daily trips to all local sites
Courses:	PADI open water to divemaster, plus specialty courses
Other:	Rota's largest selection of T-shirts; repair department

S2 Club Rota

P.O. Box 1469
Rota, MP 95951
☎ 532-3483 Fax: 532-3489

Sales & Rentals:	Limited equipment sales & rentals
Credit Cards:	Most major credit cards accepted
Air:	On-site compressor
Boats:	Daily boat dives, snorkeling tours

Sirena Marine Service Rota

P.O. Box 1340
Rota, MP 95951
☎ 532-0304 Fax: 532-0305

Sales & Rentals:	Limited equipment sales & rentals
Credit Cards:	Most major credit cards accepted
Air:	On-site compressor
Boats:	Daily boat dives, snorkeling tours

Yap

Beyond The Reef

P.O. Box 606
Yap, FSM 96943
☎ 350-3483 Fax: 350-3733

Email:	beyondthereef@mail.fm
Website:	www.diveyap.com
Sales & Rentals:	Most scuba equipment for rent or sale, including lights & cameras
Credit Cards:	Visa, Mastercard
Air:	Compressor at Pacific Islands Gas Company
Boats:	3 boats: 22 ft (5 divers), 22 ft (4 divers), 17 ft (3 divers)
Trips:	Daily 2-tank trips including night dives, free lunch & barbeques
Courses:	PADI open water to divemaster
Other:	Specialize in small groups with professional dive guides

Nature's Way

P.O. Box 238
Yap, FSM 96943
☎ 350-2542 Fax: 350-3407

Email:	naturesway@mail.fm
Sales & Rentals:	Some scuba items for sale, rentals available
Credit Cards:	Most major credit cards accepted
Air:	Filled locally
Boats:	Boats for small groups
Trips:	Daily trips to mantas and reefs
Courses:	PADI certification
Other:	Specialize in Japanese groups, but English groups welcome

Yap Divers

P.O. Box MR
Yap, FSM 96943
☎ 350-2300 Fax: 350-4567

Email:	yapdivers@mantaray.com
Website:	www.mantaray.com
Sales & Rentals:	Full scuba equipment for rent or sale
Credit Cards:	All major credit cards accepted
Air:	Nitrox & oxygen fills available, compressor on-site
Boats:	5 boats ranging in size from 4 to 20 divers
Trips:	Daily 2-tank, 3 & 4-tank trips with lunch; 1-tank afternoon macro dives and night dives
Courses:	All PADI courses, including enriched air; offers the world's only PADI specialty course on manta rays
Other:	Located & operated with the Manta Ray Bay Hotel, private gear lockers, full-service video and photo center

Tourist Services

Guam Visitor's Bureau
401 Pale Sun Vitores Road
Tumon, Guam 96911
☎ 671-646-5278
Fax: 671-646-8861.
Email: request@visitguam.com.
Website: www.visitguam.org

Mariana Visitors Bureau
P.O. Box 861
Saipan, MP 96950
☎ 670-664-3200
Fax: 670-664-3237
Email: mvb@saipan.com
Website: www.visit-marianas.com

Yap Visitors Bureau
P.O. Box 988,
Colonia, Yap FSM 96943
☎ 691-350-2298
Fax: 691-350-7015
Email: yvb@mail.fm
Website: www.VisitYap.com

Index

dive sites covered in this book appear in **bold** type

Lonely Planet Pisces Books

The **Diving & Snorkeling** books are dive guides to top destinations worldwide. Beautifully illustrated with full-color photos throughout, the series explores the best diving and snorkeling areas and prepares divers for what to expect when they get there. Each site is described in detail, with information on suggested ability levels, depth, visibility, and, of course, marine life. There's basic topside information as well for each destination. Don't miss the guides to:

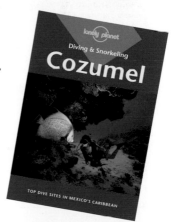

Australia: Coral Sea &
   Great Barrier Reef

Australia: Southeast Coast

Bahamas: Family Islands & Grand

Bahamas: Nassau &
   New Providence

Bali & the Komodo Region

Belize

Bermuda

Best Caribbean Diving

Bonaire

British Virgin Islands

Cayman Islands

Cocos Island

Cozumel

Cuba

Curaçao

Fiji

Florida Keys

Florida's East Coast

Guam & Yap

Hawaiian Islands

Jamaica

Northern California
   & Monterey
   Peninsula

Pacific Northwest

Palau

Puerto Rico

Red Sea

Roatan & Honduras'
   Bay Islands

Scotland

Seychelles

Southern California

St. Maarten, Saba,
   & St. Eustatius

Texas

Truk Lagoon

Turks & Caicos

U.S. Virgin Islands

Vanuatu

Plus illustrated natural history guides:

Pisces Guide to Caribbean
   Reef Ecology

Great Reefs of the World

Sharks of Tropical &
   Temperate Seas

Venomous & Toxic
   Marine Life of
   the World

Watching Fishes

Where to Find Us . . .

Lonely Planet is known worldwide for publishing practical, reliable and no-nonsense travel information in our guides and on our web site. The Lonely Planet list covers just about every accessible part of the world. Currently there are nine series: *Pisces books, travel guides, shoestring guides, walking guides, city guides, phrasebooks, audio packs, travel atlases* and *Journeys*–a unique collection of travel writing.

Lonely Planet Publications

Australia
PO Box 617, Hawthorn 3122, Victoria
☎ (03) 9819 1877 fax (03) 9819 6459
e-mail talk2us@lonelyplanet.com.au

USA
150 Linden Street
Oakland, California 94607
☎ (510) 893 8555, (800) 275 8555
fax (510) 893 8563
e-mail info@lonelyplanet.com

UK
10A Spring Place,
London NW5 3BH
☎ (0171) 428 4800 fax (0171) 428 4828
e-mail go@lonelyplanet.co.uk

France
1 rue du Dahomey
75011 Paris
☎ 01 55 25 33 00 fax 01 55 25 33 01
e-mail bip@lonelyplanet.fr

World Wide Web: www.lonelyplanet.com or **AOL keyword: lp**